THE CITY
AS METAPHOR

THE CITY
AS Metaphor

BY

DAVID R. WEIMER

Rutgers University

Random House *New York*

STUDIES IN LANGUAGE AND LITERATURE

ACKNOWLEDGMENTS

W. H. Auden: quotations reprinted are copyright and are reprinted by permission of Random House, Inc., and Faber and Faber Ltd. Quotation from "Letter to Lord Byron: Part III" reprinted by permission of the Author; copyright 1937 by W. H. Auden, copyright renewed 1964 by W. H. Auden.

Charles Baudelaire: "Rêve parisien," from *Flowers of Evil*, Harper & Row. Copyright 1936, 1963 by Edna St. Vincent Millay and Norma Millay Ellis. By permission of Norma Millay Ellis. "Morning Twilight" (*Le crépuscule du matin*) from *Flowers of Evil*, Marthiel and Jackson Mathews, eds. Transl. David Paul. Copyright 1955, 1962 by New Directions. Reprinted by permission of the publisher, New Directions.

E. E. Cummings: all quotations reprinted from his volume, *Poems 1923–1954* by permission of Harcourt, Brace & World, Inc.; Copyright 1923, 1925, 1931, 1935, 1938, 1940, 1951, 1953, 1954, 1959 by E. E. Cummings; Copyright, 1926, by Horace Liveright; Copyright, 1963, by Marion Morehouse Cummings.

Franz Kafka: excerpt from *The Trial*, transl. by Willa and Edwin Muir. Reprinted by permission of Alfred A. Knopf, Inc.

Rainer Maria Rilke: excerpt from *The Book of Hours*, transl. by A. L. Peck. Reprinted by permission of The Hogarth Press Ltd.

William Carlos Williams: quotations from *The Collected Earlier Poems*, Copyright 1938, 1951 by William Carlos Williams; from *The Collected Later Poems*, Copyright 1944, 1948, 1950, and 1963 by Wm. C. Williams; from *Patterson*, Copyright © 1946, 1948, 1949, 1951, 1958 by Wm. C. Williams, Copyright © 1963 by Florence Williams, and from *Pictures from Brueghel and Other Poems*, Copyright 1949, 1954, 1962 by Wm. C. Williams, reprinted by permission of the publisher, New Directions Publishing Corporation.

James Wright: "The Year Changes in the City," © 1960, by Harper's Magazine, Inc., reprinted by permission of the author.

Library of Congress Catalog Card Number: 66–15812
Manufactured in the United States of America by
The Colonial Press, Clinton, Mass.

Preface

A book published some thirty years ago on the city in nineteenth-century American novels included a chapter with the title, "Disasters of City Life." There the author faithfully reported instances in these novels of City Plagues or Epidemics, Duelling, Intemperance, Poverty, and Villainy. The fact helps illustrate what I do not attempt here.

Designed as a critical introduction to major American writers on the city, this book has both the broad and narrow aims which that description implies. In it I wish to point out neglected features of that native poetry and fiction in which the city figures prominently as theme or image, and I wish also to present that body of work to the reader broadly in the light of this particular focus. My leading concern is with the figurative uses to which the metropolis has been put, with the language in which it has been fixed.

The question governing my choice of authors has been: *Does the writer advance our awareness of 'the city'?* The answers to this question have led me to omit such contemporaries as Dos Passos, Farrell, and Algren. Hart Crane and Eliot are absent for different reasons. Apart from fragmentary observations, I have nothing to add to existing criticism of *The Bridge*. Only "The Tunnel" section, moreover, seems to me to bear in any but a general or tangential way on an identifiably urban theme; the center of the poem is, variously considered, America, the modern technological world, myth, the poet's creative self. Aspects of Eliot's Unreal City I do allude to here and there, but its significance in *The Waste Land* has been more or less exhaustively appraised. Such earlier cities as the New York of Melville's *Pierre,* the Rome of Hawthorne's *The Marble Faun,* or even the Philadelphia of Charles Brockden Brown's *Wieland* and the San Francisco of Norris' *McTeague* all have their points of literary interest, as do any number of other tales and poems not treated here; but the merits of examining a few writers in some detail have appeared to me to outweigh those of comprehensiveness.

I regret that Donald Fanger's excellent study of Dostoevsky, Balzac, Dickens, and Gogol—*Dostoevsky and Romantic Realism* (Harvard University Press, 1965)—which emphasizes their treatments of the city, was published too late for me to take it into account as I should have liked. His comparative analysis is exactly one of the kinds requisite for the reader's knowledge of literary cities other than those created by Americans. His book can help, therefore, to correct any imbalance produced by the oppressive parochialism of a study like my own that follows national boundaries.

I wish to thank Elizabeth Bishop and Lota de Maçedo Soares for their generosity with books and working-space at a time when I needed both badly, and for their friendly interest in this study. The manuscript itself has profited most from criticism by Paul Fussell, Jr., who has stimulated, encouraged, and disciplined my judgments in just the right proportion from the outset, and by Mark Spilka, who has aided me as well by the high standards of his own published work.

In addition, I am grateful to the staff of the Rutgers University Library for assistance of various kinds over the years, and to the Rutgers Research Council for a grant-in-aid that facilitated the completion of this book. Mrs. Anne McCartney handled the typing with exemplary skill and fidelity.

D.R.W.

Contents

Introduction: *American Writers and the City*   1

(I)   *Mast-Hemm'd Mannahatta:* WALT WHITMAN   14
(II)   *Babylons Visited:* HENRY JAMES   34
(III) *Landscape of Hysteria:* STEPHEN CRANE   52
(IV) *Heathen Catacombs:* THEODORE DREISER   65
(V)   *Grassblades Assassinated:* E. E. CUMMINGS   78
(VI) *Lost City:* F. SCOTT FITZGERALD   88
(VII) *Two Cities:* WILLIAM CARLOS WILLIAMS 104
(VIII) *Rome Sacked:* W. H. AUDEN   123

Epilogue: *The City Today*   144

Suggested Readings   147
Index   149

To Pat

Introduction:
American Writers and the City

At the age of eighteen, living in the parish of East Windsor, Connecticut, Jonathan Edwards felt the spirit stirring within him that was to lead to his conversion. "My sense of divine things seemed gradually to increase," he revealed in the *Personal Narrative*, "till I went to preach at New York, which was about a year and a half after they began; and while I was there, I felt them very sensibly, in a much higher degree than I had done before." The conversion itself occurred in New York, then a town of some seven thousand persons, following months of self-abasement, weeping, and solitary walks "on the banks of Hudson's River, at some distance from the city, for contemplation on divine things and secret converse with God. . . ." This critical visit lasted but a few months, after which Edwards returned to his rural Connecticut home. Twenty years later, he could still remember his grief at the departure:

I came away from New York in the month of April, 1723, and had a most bitter parting with Madam Smith and her son. My heart seemed to sink within me, at leaving the family and city, where I had enjoyed so many sweet and pleasant days. I went from New York to Wethersfield, by water; and as I sailed away, I kept sight of the city as long as I could.

Over the next two and a half centuries countless Americans were to feel comparable sensations at leaving "the city," at arriving, at confronting it in any one of a thousand ways. In time New York and the other centers would expand and tower, so that to all but the most rustic inhabitants of the land a place of a few thousand souls would seem paltry indeed. But as the Edwards account suggests, size might matter very little, or only relatively. What did matter, to nearly every impressionable spirit from colonial days on, was the shape of his own encounter with what he thought of as the city; and when gifted native poets and novelists appeared in the second quarter of the nineteenth century, they gave these encounters imaginative identity and so a life beyond that of the private or merely literal record.

Of course they gave them numerous identities. For while the cities imagined by Whitman, Stephen Crane, and the others have both historical and representative elements, faithful to fact and to the American experience at large, each is also to some degree autonomous and unique. Self-evident as this point may seem to students of literature, it bears emphasis. Commentators on the cities of American literature persistently assume that the artist's task has been at bottom reportorial. But while Jonathan Edwards' desire to keep the city in view as long as he could may be interpreted satisfactorily on psychological and historical grounds, these grounds quite give way when we come to the opening chapter of *Moby-Dick*, where Ishmael relates his haunting vision of water-gazing men by the thousands lining miles of Manhattan waterfront, "posted like silent sentinels all around the town . . . fixed in ocean reveries." Nor can biography or history tell us much about a line from "Song of Myself" such as that in which "we" are represented as

entering by the suburbs some vast and ruined city. . . .

And though some knowledge of the traditional moral repute attaching popularly to modern Paris and ancient Babylon helps us to understand James's *The Ambassadors* or Fitzgerald's "Babylon Revisited" or even Bellow's *Henderson the Rain King,* the cities in these works of fiction derive their significance *primarily* from within the individual works themselves. 'Babylon' (in the Bellow novel, 'Ur') is not precisely the same thing from one of these tales to the other, and neither is 'Paris.'

A recognition of this general truth about literary cities has been delayed because of a lingering naïveté on difficult yet elementary questions about the way art works. This naïveté is always abroad in the streets and need cause little alarm so long as the inexperienced are continually learning the special disciplines of art and so coming to respect them. One takes alarm, though, when established scholars fail of either the learning or the respect. Regrettably, one or both failures have characterized the description of American literary cities to date, on the part of literary and nonliterary specialists alike. The most recent example comes, as it happens, from the latter group—*The Intellectual versus the City* (1962) by Morton and Lucia White. Because their book demonstrates so well which 'cities' have *not* been significant in American literature and so points, by implication, to those that have, it deserves our brief preliminary attention.

The Whites set out to "describe, analyze, and classify . . . intellectual reactions to the American city"—a perfectly sound type of historical inquiry. The subject matter of their inquiry, however, is the published work not just of social critics, historians, philosophers, and sociologists but of poets and novelists as well. The conceivably baffling question of how *attitudes* toward the city are to be elicited from the poetry and fiction of such writers as Melville, Poe, and Henry James finds in this study two answers: by dealing with poems, stories, and novels containing explicit statements about the city, and by going outside belletristic materials to the evidence of essays, notebooks, and correspondence. Thus the Whites take up Poe's "The City in the Sea," a short poem in which, as they say, "a city is buried by water"; they quote lines of a direct nature—

> No rays from the holy heaven come down
> On the long night-time of that town . . .

—commenting that "the whole scene is ghostly and filmy"; then they observe that "we are not told by the poet what town this is" but cite a source indicating that the town is probably to be identified (from names given in another poem, "Al Araaf") as Tadmor, Persepolis, Balbec, or Gomorrah. Elsewhere the authors note that *The Marble Faun* "contains a catalogue of anti-urban expletives," which they forthwith list, contenting themselves by way of additional comment on that novel with brief observations on the preface, the thematic function of Rome, the tower and plain symbolism (promising but undeveloped), and Hawthorne's very quotable assertion that "all towns should be made capable of purification by fire, or of decay, within each half-century."

As in their treatment of Henry James—whose cities in *The American, The Ambassadors,* "Daisy Miller," and *The Portrait of a Lady* they pass over for his scattered remarks on cities in the notebooks, letters, travel essays, *The American Scene,* and *The Princess Casamassima*—the Whites persistently shy away from the more enigmatic literary works. At the same time, their refusal to deal with riddles, for the most part even to acknowledge the presence of riddle, has its own consistency, because they do not think of literature as *essentially* different from history or philosophy. Their view is pretty much the layman's view: a poem is just prose decorated, a story is an idea dramatized. The poem or novel is thus largely indistinguishable from the essay or the personal letter, except perhaps in being more interestingly written. From this perspective it seems logical—or at least not strange—

to ignore complexities in a work of art, to by-pass the interpretive difficulties of coming at literary cities through the
fabric of metaphor, the nuances of tone.

An analysis comparable in this respect to the Whites' (to
mention one other example only) is to be found in a volume
of essays edited by Oscar Handlin and John Burchard, *The
Historian and the City* (1963). There the admirable essay by
Carl E. Schorske on "The Idea of the City in European
Thought: Voltaire to Spengler" proceeds smoothly—as the
Whites' chapters on such thinkers as Henry Adams generally
proceed—until it dips into literary 'evidence.' Then we realize that only a certain type of source is being presented to us,
as in the lines Schorske quotes from Blake,

> I wander thro' each charter'd street,
> Near where the charter'd Thames does flow,
> And mark in every face I meet
> Marks of weakness, marks of woe[,]

or in these taken from Rilke:

> But cities seek their own, not others' good;
> they drag all with them in their headlong haste.
> They smash up animals like hollow wood
> and countless nations they burn up for waste.*

The main theme of each of these stanzas has the virtue of
explicitness. But is it for that reason more important as a
comment on the city than a theme which is merely intimated,
as in the following poem?

> I see nothing before me
> But the dark wing
> Of a policeman,
> And I hear nothing
> But a violet
> Dragging its chains.

* In the translation by A. L. Peck (London, 1961).

> It is only underground that I hear
> The muffled cry of a tree,
> A vixen laboring to bear
> Ghosts in her sleep.

> (James Wright, "The Year Changes in the City")

Not more important—one should like everyone to agree—only more efficiently understood, and therefore resorted to only when the treatment of a complex literary work on its own terms proves impracticable.

In this book, then, we turn from the recorded to the created, from cities described to cities perceived. Even Dreiser's Chicago and William Carlos Williams' Paterson—two literary cities built more entirely from the materials of history than, say, the New York of Whitman's poems—even these have been abundantly wrought, fashioned, made over. The categories we *most* require in order to deal with these cities are therefore not historical, sociological, or epistemological but metaphoric. The difference becomes clearest on the very point which the Whites and indeed most literary historians take most for granted—that the city is objectively real, and that American writers have all been either philosophic Realists (facing up to their urban-industrial environment) or solipsists (escaping into dream). But Whitman and Crane and the others are forever placing the question of its reality in doubt. To speak more appropriately and exactly, they seldom wonder whether the city is real, but they wonder perpetually whether it is *solid,* which is to say prosaic, identifiable, or unambiguous.

Approached thus through metaphor, the cities invented by American poets and novelists impress by their diversity. There are as many cities as there are imaginations. Since the demonstration of this variety is left to the pages ahead, we may look instead for a moment at some of the principal features which these fictive cities exhibit in common.

Of these features, a few reappear most often and interestingly. One emerges at the outset in Whitman's poetry, a quality which for convenience we may name simply *the miraculous*. Although Whitman does sometimes treat cities as phenomena merely, as in the gazetteer sections of "Salut au Monde!," his better poems transform them into "gliding wonders," and Manhattan nearly always appears to him strangely evanescent, rescued but momentarily by language from the mysterious flux of time and place.

> . . . heaven-clouds canopy my city with a delicate thin haze. . . .

> What gods can exceed these that clasp me by the hand . . . ?

The great solvent of miracle is of course knowledge; and those American city writers who respond to the first usually interest themselves also in how precariously it lives in the face of the second. Only for Whitman does a sense of the miraculous in the city never quite dissolve, not even under the "curious abrupt questionings" that move the observer of Manhattan in "Crossing Brooklyn Ferry," or under the awareness of "a secret silent loathing and despair" behind the "window-pierc'd façades" of the cities in "Song of the Open Road." Had he written any New York poems of consequence after his return there in 1870, the disenchantment they might have shown is suggested by the famous passage in *Democratic Vistas* where he delivers his moral and aesthetic indictment of New York and Brooklyn as "a sort of dry and flat Sahara." This intrusion of the critical intellect is somewhat offset, however, by Whitman's impassioned tribute in the preceding paragraph to the "Splendor, picturesqueness, and oceanic amplitude and rush of these great cities" and by his succeeding declaration of optimism for the renewal there of "sane and heroic life."

Precisely the loss of wonder through knowledge was to be expressed by F. Scott Fitzgerald, in his evocative prose reminiscence, "My Lost City":

From the ruins, lonely and inexplicable as the sphinx, rose
the Empire State Building and, just as it had been a tradition of mine to climb to the Plaza Roof to take leave of the
beautiful city, extending as far as eyes could reach, so now
I went to the roof of the last and most magnificent of
towers. Then I understood—everything was explained: I
had discovered the crowning error of the city, its Pandora's
box. Full of vaunting pride the New Yorker had climbed
here and seen with dismay what he had never suspected,
that the city was not the endless succession of canyons
that he had supposed but that *it had limits*—from the tall-
est structure he saw for the first time that it faded out into
the country on all sides, into an expanse of green and blue
that alone was limitless. And with the awful realization
that New York was a city after all and not a universe, the
whole shining edifice that he had reared in his imagination
came crashing to the ground.

The intent of this striking passage is to suggest the author's
disillusion—with New York itself, with his life generally.
The city had been magical, and it was no longer. *It had
limits.* Mystery had evaporated, wonders had turned into
solids. And yet, as in *Democratic Vistas,* somehow surviving
the artist's moment of "realization" is an after-image of
illimitable city splendor.

The balance of mystery against consciousness is shown to
be fragile in Cummings also, as in this fragment from a
poem of the 1940 collection: "cities may overflow . . . /as-
sassinating whole grassblades. . . ." Here the quiet effectiveness of the flood metaphor—magnificently apt for a great
city and unobtrusive—is shattered by the word "assassinat-
ing," which *demands* analysis. The poet's intellectuality has
barged in, requiring that ours follow. Working toward a
similarly disruptive end is the pattern of imagery established
in William Carlos Williams' poem, "Perpetuum Mobile: The
City," where the city is first evoked as attractively mysterious—

> At night
> > it wakes
> On the black
> > sky—
>
> a dream
> > toward which
> we love—

and is then abruptly subjected to realistic judgment:

> at night
> > more
> than a little
> > false. . . .

The "magnet" that shows up in the initial chapter title of *Sister Carrie* and that subsequently becomes one of Dreiser's favorite analogies for the metropolis has properties at once occult and scientifically describable—an anomaly perfectly suited to the author's half-entranced, half-naturalistic vision of the cities his characters inhabit. And in James's fiction, most formidably in *The Ambassadors,* historical and other mysteries hang awesomely over Continental cities in thick curtains the protagonists must pass through as a condition of their journey toward fuller consciousness.

Stephen Crane is a special case, easily misread. In a way, his first long Bowery tale depends for its chief impact on scenes showing how Maggie's slum *destroys* all sense of the marvelous. But a sense of wonder is not exactly the alternative Crane offers to this destruction. For him the city is not even potentially miraculous, it is fantastic. Not given like Whitman and Fitzgerald to finding unusual powers in the object, Crane perceived the city instead as an extension of the psyche. Some such projective or extensive conception of the metropolis is a second element common to some of the literary cities.

The element least often seen, it is one of the most interesting. While certain projective impulses lie behind all art, they dominate the results only in some. Among modern novelists we think first of Kafka, the stairways and chambers of whose cities seem the direct counterparts of passageways and compartments in his own mind; among poets, of Baudelaire, whose fears take the form of seven old men met on the streets of a spectral city (*Fourmillante cité, cité pleine de rêves*), or in whose nightmarish "Parisian Dream" there rises a moonless, sunless, silent city without vegetation or human beings:

> And, proud of what my art had done,
> I viewed my painting, knew the great
> Intoxicating monotone
> Of marble, water, steel and slate.*

That Eliot's Unreal City of *The Waste Land* owes something to Baudelaire's "swarming city" (as Eliot intimates in a note to the first section) but that we can deduce little of psychological consequence from the Eliot image suggests that exceptional artistry may serve either to reveal or to screen the unconscious. The comparative visibility of a writer's psychic landscape seems to depend on an essentially psychological, rather than artistic, naïveté or candor. Thus while we may agree with Quentin Anderson that Henry James's 'America' and 'Europe' represent aspects of James's mind, it is difficult (notoriously!) to identify those aspects in any but very general terms, whereas a more confessional writer such as Stephen Crane scatters clues to his specific private agonies all over the imaginary terrain. Closest to Crane in this respect, among the American city artists, is Williams, whose Paterson and New York stand out from his poems as emblems of his own deep disquiet.

---

* Translated by Edna St. Vincent Millay. The original reads:

> *Et, peintre fier de mon génie,*
> *Je savourais dans mon tableau*
> *L'enivrante monotonie*
> *Du métal, du marbre et de l'eau.*

Still another perception of 'the city,' alongside the miraculous and the projective, shows up in the difference between Williams' lines about New York,

> For years I've been tormented by
> that miracle . . . ,

and these by Auden:

> Across East River in the night
> Manhattan is ablaze with light.

In this instance, the key to Williams' city is a word—not "miracle," as it happens, but "tormented." The key to Auden's city, on the other hand, is to be found in the conventionality of his verse form. To Auden, the city means the organization of social experience, moral or civil *order*. There is an element of the visionary about his city, but he does not find it intrinsically magical; an element also of the psychic, but it does not carry us securely down through subterranean levels of his mind. Next to Whitman's city in particular, Auden's seems all cold-blooded knowledge, intellect, idea. Here is the consciousness before which miracle withers, beneath which the buried life remains buried. Or largely so: one speaks necessarily of tendencies, identifies through contrast. Were his city purely idea, without aura or depth, it would not become as it so often does a part of that "memorable speech" Auden hoped to write. But wonder does reside in lines like these which open "The Shield of Achilles":

> She looked over his shoulder
> For vines and olive trees,
> Marble well-governed cities . . .

and a responsiveness to mystery is to be felt even in his abstract evocations through various poems of "the Just City."*

* Randall Jarrell's well-known and impressive critique of recurrent psychological themes in Auden's work (*Partisan Review*, 1945)

The metropolis represents a different kind of order to
James, whose Paris, Florence, Rome, and (sometimes) London speak of the traditional and partially desirable cultiva-
tion of sensibility, broadly conceived, as distinct from the
anarchic disregard for form, the amorphous taste, conspicu-
ous in America. Refinement both limits and releases, the
Isabel Archers and Lambert Strethers learn; order may un-
settle. Their cities prove thus endlessly ambiguous. In Fitzgerald, too, the city stands for the subjection of experience
to form—not as a theme, however, but as a technical ideal,
and in comparison with James's city a good deal less con-
sciously recognized as having a role in his fiction. The New
York so prominent as subject matter in Fitzgerald's work
really proves, once we become aware of this other 'city,' to
occupy quite a secondary place. Cummings' New York, on
the other hand, supplies form and subject alike. Fortuitously
—and ironically—the poetic techniques he seizes upon to
subdue the metropolis are suggested by the victim.

For some of the writers, the urban connotes order of yet
another species—order unwittingly arrived at, knowledge or
conditions imposed, in a word *fate*. " 'I always feel doomed
when the train is running into London,' " one character says
hopelessly to another in a modern English novel—an admis-
sion that might stand in its general implications as the epi-
graph to any number of American as well as English novels
of the city. The statement is made by Rupert Birkin in
Women in Love and has just enough of the author's sympathy behind it to make us take it seriously. London is dead
humanity, mankind in the mass, calculation, Sodom, "real
death." Lawrence might have been speaking for certain
Americans who have shared the spirit of his individualist
theme if not his particular formulation of it. In the proximity
of mechanism the organic life suffers; social constraint, great

---

demonstrates the applicability of that kind of analysis to the work of
even the most self-conscious poet. Auden's 'city' by itself does not,
however, point very directly toward these themes.

impersonal forces doom the free and spontaneous individual. The idea is as mysterious in its own way as the perception of the city as full of marvels, but the overtones are wholly sinister. The doom is simplest and most explainable for Stephen Crane's Bowery inhabitants, nearly as simple if less immediate for the self-indulgent proletarians in the public park of Williams' *Paterson*. The feeling of fatality is strongest in Dreiser, whose protagonists find that once they enter the city, circumstances close so tightly around them as to allow no exit of any kind. And in James also the note sounds clearly, on the lips of his men and women, in the transcendent necessity that seems at times to impel them to the discoveries they make in Paris or Rome, despite the large freedom of action with which they are endowed.

Except in the loosest sense, of course, this recurrent imagery of miracle and fantasy, of order and fate, does not form a literary tradition. Until quite recently, when American writers generally have shown an increasing dependence on their predecessors, links between the various city writers have been decidedly tenuous. The connections have in the main been minor and fragmentary, seen only in a moment like that when Fitzgerald's Anthony Patch faces the very mansions so revered by Dreiser's heroes and passes a quite different judgment on them, or in the passages where Williams invokes the myths of New World promise that Whitman had helped fashion, though for the purpose of deploring how far that promise had suffered debasement in the modern metropolis. The 'city' of American literature is thus several cities, whose meaning and appeal derive first of all from their singularity.

Mast-Hemm'd Mannahatta

WALT WHITMAN

Whitman was to recall in *Specimen Days* that the Brooklyn of his childhood and youth had been "thoroughly rural." It acquired an urban character in the very years he was learning how to convert experience into poetry, but for Whitman it never rivaled the greater island city across the East River. New York was "the great place of the western continent, the heart, the brain, the focus, the main spring, the pinnacle, the extremity, the no more beyond, of the New World. . . ." While he would eventually shed the unskillfulness of hyperbole shown in this panegyric from the New York *Aurora,* written when Whitman was twenty-three, he would keep the hyperbole. Other journalistic pieces and later his reminiscences reveal how exhilarating he found New York, which he customarily spoke of as "my city" and was to re-create as *Mannahatta.* But his excitement is most compelling in his poetry, and it is for that rather than for his occasional journalism that we do, after all, return to him.

It was a writer of the next century, "tormented" by that metropolitan spectacle from a different shore, who was to think of a poem as "an assertion, always, of a new and total culture, the lifting of an environment to expression." William Carlos Williams might have had Whitman in mind, who lifted so many American environments to expression. Among these, as we all know, were the open road and the seashore, with which our first poet remains largely identified; but among them also was the city, toward which both Whitman's life and imagination turned as easily, pleasurably, and impressively.

One or another image of Mannahatta dominates many of his best short poems and portions of several longer ones, while other cities and "cities" in general turn up throughout his poetry, from the first edition of the *Leaves* in 1855 to verses written shortly before he died. Of his major pieces only "Out of the Cradle" and "Passage to India" fail to introduce the subject in some way. A number, including "Song of Myself," contain passages whose appreciation depends partly on an awareness of Whitman's imaginings of the city, and all kinds of fragments come clearer under this new light. "He thought of himself both as the poet of the city and as the poet of nature," F. O. Matthiessen once observed, and he contrasted Whitman's outlook in this respect with that of Wordsworth or Baudelaire, noting how "remote" the American's "eager abandonment to sprawling New York in its iron age was . . . from Baudelaire's haunted sense of the oppression of the metropolis upon the lonely individual." The contrast is warranted, but it presupposes a simpler 'city' and a simpler involvement with that city than Whitman's poetry in fact discloses. What that body of work does show is the poet approaching the city from varying distances and perspectives, making poetic use of it with the remarkable versatility that characterized his best efforts, forging identities for an object too new to American life and too amorphous to have received sharp prior definition.

In the *Enfans d'Adam* section beginning "Once I pass'd through a populous city," the speaker tells of "imprinting my brain, for future use, with its shows, architecture, customs, and traditions. . . ." Whether or not the place was

New Orleans or the date 1848, the statement looks suffi-
ciently authentic as a confession of Whitman's own ran-
domly acquisitive curiosity during that early period. Although his backward glances are always suspect, particularly
when embedded in poems, it sounds exactly like the inquisi-
tive young traveler to have been loading his knapsack fur-
tively with impressions for an obscure "future use." When
the time came to unload, it was characteristic of him also
to puzzle where to set everything down, but to be confident
that it would all find its proper place. The city hoardings
that we find in his earliest poems sometimes impress us as
having been stacked there temporarily, awaiting better use.
"Do you enjoy yourself in the city?" he asks innocently in
one of the shorter 1855 poems,

> or engaged in business? or planning a
> nomination and election? or with your wife and
> family?
> Or with your mother and sisters? or in womanly
> housework? or the beautiful maternal cares?

The initial line of the stanza supplies the category for this
apparently indiscriminate cluster: "To think how much pleasure there is!" It is a loose category. Here, as at most other
points in the first *Leaves of Grass,* the city is simply another
notation from experience. But the frequency and concreteness
of these city entries, particularly in "Song of Myself," testify
to the liveliness of Whitman's interest in them. *By the city's
quadrangular houses . . . Approaching Manhattan . . . Looking in at the shop-windows in Broadway . . . They who piddle
and patter there in collars and tailed coats . . . My lovers . . .
[j]ostling me through streets and public halls . . . flagging
of sidewalks by flaggers . . . the ladders and hanging ropes of
the gymnasium . . . the bonfire of shavings in the open lot in
the city . . . the crowd of children watching*—all these from
a much larger number of brief references—and then the long
stanza from the eighth chant which begins,

> The blab of the pave. . . . the tires of carts and sluff of
> bootsoles and talk of the promenaders,
> The heavy omnibus, the driver with his interrogating
> thumb, the clank of the shod horses on the granite
> floor. . . .

Manhattan (which we may assume inspired most of them) thus gave Whitman at the outset some of his most vivid lines. Surely it enabled him to imagine sounding his barbaric yawp "over the roofs of the world." At the same time, these colorful pieces are—just pieces, as though Whitman were carefully rotating a kaleidoscope, looking for patterns.

Then abruptly in 1856, in the way he had (after whatever gestation) of suddenly arriving at his subject, the city patterns appear. One of these shows a kind of tracery over the surface of the globe. "Salut au Monde!" tells of steamships that

> Wait at Liverpool, Glasgow, Dublin, Marseilles, Lis-
> bon, Naples, Hamburg, Bremen, Bordeaux, the
> Hague, Copenhagen,
> Wait at Valparaiso, Rio Janeiro, Panama. . . .
>
> I see the cities of the earth, and make myself at random
> a part of them,
> I am a real Parisian,
> I am a habitan of Vienna,* St. Petersburg, Berlin, Con-
> stantinople,
> I am of Adelaide, Sidney, Melbourne,
> I am of London, Manchester, Bristol, Edinburg,
> Limerick,

then after cities of the Iberian peninsula, France, Belgium, Switzerland, Germany, Italy, Russia, Poland, and Scandinavia, Whitman passes on to Africa and Asia:

---

* Randall Jarrell says of this wonderful phrase: "One has an immediate vision of him as a sort of French-Canadian halfbreed to whom the Viennese are offering, with trepidation, through the bars of a zoological garden, little mounds of whipped cream."

I see Algiers, Tripoli, Derne, Mogadore, Timbuctoo,
   Monrovia,
I see the swarms of Pekin, Canton, Benares, Delhi,
   Calcutta, Yedo,

and so on. Here cities are "gliding wonders," exotic names,
remote places, the mysterious, Romance. They are also parti-
cles, phenomena, implying a transcendental metaphysics:
"Such joined unended links, each hooked to the next!/Each
answering all—each sharing the earth with all."

But while he asserted in a closing line that "What cities
the light or warmth penetrates, I penetrate those cities myself," "Salut au Monde!" did not itself effect any real pene-
tration. The Romantic or metaphysical significance of its
cities lies exactly at the level of the "ranks, colors, barbarisms, civilizations" and all the other orders of the poem.
That absolute parallelism of phenomena has of course its
own enormous interest in any analysis of Whitman's aesthet-
ics or politics. But its effectiveness and therefore a part of its
meaning depends, paradoxically, on its dissolution—on the
poet's breaking up this atomistic egalitarianism either by dis-
criminating among its parts or by subjecting some to more
impassioned scrutiny than others. As Whitman refrains from
making any such distinctions in his salute to cities, these fur-
nish us with little insight into anything.

The kind of perception afforded by proximity to the object is shown in another poem of the same year. "Poem of the
Road" (later retitled "Song of the Open Road"), whose
thrust is directly away from the city, manages by a sort of
counterthrust to enter it. Here for the first time Whitman
makes the city significant in a poem of some length. He identifies it principally with the Indoors that we are urged to quit.
It means "the old smooth prizes," arbitrary limitations, arti-
ficiality, pleasure, disease, convenience, shelter, repose and
custom—as opposed to the Outdoors of heroic opportunity,
expansiveness, freedom, health, self-fulfillment, love, joy,

the untried and difficult, "active rebellion." Both the ringing
and the sentention lines through which Whitman calls us to
the highway are well known: "I think heroic deeds were all
conceived in the open air . . . Allons! The road is before us!"
Less noticed, retiring as it were before the clamorous open-
road histrionics, is the passionate gloom of his innermost indoors, introduced near the beginning of the poem with this
vigorous apostrophe:

> You flagged walks of the cities! you strong curbs at the
>   edges! . . .
> You rows of houses! you window-pierced façades! you
>   roofs!
> You porches and entrances! you copings and iron
>   guards!
> You windows whose transparent shells might expose so
>   much!

What the windows might expose is revealed in the forceful
passage near the end:

> . . . Out of the dark confinement!
> It is useless to protest—I know all, and expose it.
> Behold, through you as bad as the rest,
> Through the laughter, dancing, dining, supping, of
>   people,
> Inside of dresses and ornaments, inside of those washed
>   and trimmed faces,
> Behold a secret silent loathing and despair.
>
> No husband, no wife, no friend, no lover, so trusted as
>   to hear the confession,
> Another self, a duplicate of every one, skulking and
>   hiding it goes, open and above board it goes,
> Formless and wordless through the streets of the cities,
>   polite and bland in the parlors,
> In the cars of rail-roads, in steam-boats, in the public
>   assembly,

Home to the houses of men and women, among their
    families, at the table, in the bed-room, everywhere,
Smartly attired, countenance smiling, form upright,
    death under the breast-bones, hell under the skull-
    bones. . . .

This is hardly the passage Matthiessen had in mind when he
spoke of Whitman's remoteness from Baudelaire's "haunted
sense" of urban surroundings. Admittedly, Whitman does
not attribute the individual's despair to "the oppression of
the metropolis," which was Matthiessen's point of comparison between the two poets; but then neither does Baudelaire.
The three or four poems from *Les Fleurs du Mal* most comparable to Whitman's juxtapositions of city surface with
human reality—*Le Crépuscule du Soir, Le Crépuscule du
Matin, Les Sept Vieillards* and possibly *Rêve Parisien*—all
present a city whose melancholy does not at all provoke the
individual's mood but instead corresponds to it. In *Le Crépuscule du Matin,*

Here and there a house sent up a thin smoke.
Women of the streets, sunk in stupid sleep,
Seemed all raw eyelid, and gasping lip.*

This expressive treatment of environment is itself neatly
suggested by a double image from *Les Sept Vieillards: décor
semblable à l'âme de l'acteur,/Un brouillard sale et jaune
inondait tout l'espace*—the setting matched the actor's soul,/
A dirty yellow fog flooded all space. Whitman is nowhere
in his poetry so entirely committed as Baudelaire to this
particular symbolic method, but their indirectness and pessi-
mism here come extremely close together. And there is a
further similarity in the quality of their perception. "It is
not merely in the use of imagery of common life, not merely

* From the David Paul translation. The French text reads:
    Les maisons çà et là commençaient à fumer.
    Les femmes de plaisir, la paupière livide,
    Bouche ouverte, dormaient de leur sommeil stupide. . . .

in the use of imagery of the sordid life of a great metropolis, but in the elevation of such imagery to the *first intensity*—presenting it as it is, and yet making it represent something much more than itself—that [he] has created a mode of release and expression for other men." This judgment is, as it happens, Eliot's on Baudelaire, but the comment also applies extraordinarily to the American poet who found behind "window-pierced façades" a "secret silent loathing and despair."

Whitman's city of cheerless or menacing interiors turns up fragmentarily in other poems—in "Song of Myself," for example, with the suicide who "sprawls on the bloody floor of the bedroom," with the "lonesome" voyeuristic young woman who peers at the twenty-eight men bathing as she "hides, handsome and richly drest aft the blinds of the window," with the "mashed fireman" whose breast-bone is broken as "tumbling walls buried me in their debris," with the frequently furtive overtones of indoors love-making (strongest of course in the Calamus poems) and the poet's reiterated and strangely urgent insistence on the virtues of life outdoors. He is always demanding, in a sense, that we "Unscrew the locks from the doors!/Unscrew the doors themselves from their jambs!"

And yet his great impulse is not to dismantle the city but to air it out, to destroy shame by publishing the common urges of all men and women, to awaken—exactly as Emerson and Thoreau hoped to awaken—their willingness to dispense with their dwellings rather than submitting to imprisonment in them. At the same time, to recall Whitman's kinship with the New England agrarians is to recognize how enormous a distance, even in the mid-nineteenth century, separated Brooklyn from Concord. For one thing, Whitman shows little of the reverence for hoeing one's own beans that could produce a *Walden* or the more full-blown agrarianism of Emerson's essay on farming. In his 1874 poem on "The Ox-Tamer," whom Whitman describes as "my farmer friend," what begins ostensibly as eulogy of a sort of Paul Bunyan ("He will take the wildest steer in the world and break him and tame him") and of his splendid animals comes to this anti-climactic end:

> I confess I envy only his fascination—my silent, illiterate friend,
> Whom a hundred oxen love there in his life on farms,
> In the northern country far, in the placid pastoral region.

Emerson had said of the farmer, in a completely different spirit: "he stands well on the world—as Adam did, as an Indian does, as Homer's heroes, Agamemnon or Achilles, do."

More importantly, neither Waldo nor his disciple had either the convictions or the sensibility that would have permitted them to exult in the city, positively to glory in it, as Whitman did. It would have been inconceivable for the New Englanders to think of the city as representing *life*, but for Whitman it represented just that. The city is the conventional and secretive, but it is dominantly and compellingly a human spectacle, involvement, color, stir. In this he is least Baudelairean and most himself. *When million-footed Manhattan unpent descends to her pavements . . . The pavingman leans on his twohanded rammer—the reporter's lead flies swiftly over the notebook—the signpainter is lettering with red and gold . . . Approaching Manhattan up by the long-stretching island:* these are the most characteristic moments. Whitman is forever advancing toward the city, or leaving it, or watching as it streams past him. "I have always had a passion for ferries," he confided to his public in *Specimen Days.* The confession was both major and superfluous; its poetic truth is demonstrable everywhere in his city verse. There images abound of wharves, ships and harbors seen from ferries, of the city glimpsed at various removes from its periphery. He revived the "aboriginal name" of *Manna-*

hatta for the city he knew best, he implied in three lines from 1888, because it signified "A rocky founded island—shores where ever gayly dash the coming, going, hurrying sea waves." In the earlier, longer poem also entitled "Mannahatta" he explained what he liked about the name:

> Because I see that word nested in nests of water-bays,
>   superb, with tall and wonderful spires,
> Rich, hemmed thick all around with sailships and
>   steamships. . . .

"Crossing Brooklyn Ferry," published also in 1856, captures best of any single poem Whitman's view of the city at its perimeter. In the East River crossing lies the geographical center of the poem, with "the shipping of Manhattan north and west, and the heights of Brooklyn to the south and east." The objective experience to which the "I" of the poem responds is presented most completely in the seventh and eighth of the original twenty-six sections. The chief themes of the poem flow into and out of this third section, and are most fully understood in terms of it. Addressing all the future generations who will have the same experience, the speaker (a passenger) describes detail by detail this city-harbor scene, nearly suspended in time and yet strongly expressing movement:

> I too many and many a time crossed the river, the sun
>   half an hour high,
> I watched the Twelfth Month sea-gulls—I saw them
>   high in the air, floating with motionless wings, oscil-
>   lating their bodies,
> I saw how the glistening yellow lit up parts of their
>   bodies, and left the rest in strong shadow,
> I saw the slow-wheeling circles, and the gradual edging
>   toward the south.
>
> I too saw the reflection of the summer sky in the water,
> Had my eyes dazzled by the shimmering track of beams,

Looked at the fine centrifugal spokes of light round
the shape of my head in the sun-lit water . . . ,
Looked toward the lower bay to notice the arriving
ships,
Saw their approach, saw aboard those that were near
me,
Saw the white sails of schooners and sloops, saw the
ships at anchor,
The sailors at work in the rigging, or out astride the
spars . . . ,

The white wake left by the passage, the quick tremulous whirl of the wheels . . . ,

The stretch afar growing dimmer and dimmer, the gray
walls of the granite store-houses by the docks,
On the river the shadowy group, the big steam-tug
closely flanked on each side by the barges—the hay-
boat, the belated lighter,
On the neighboring shore, the fires from the foundry
chimneys burning high and glaringly into the night,
Casting their flicker of black, contrasted with wild red
and yellow light, over the tops of houses, and down
into the clefts of streets.

The gulls, the reflected sunlight, the boats, the warehouses
and the foundry fires glaring at night over the houses and
streets all interest the speaker, he implies, mainly because
they will also interest passengers to come. Confidence in
their future enjoyment of the same experience is confidence
that all human individuals belong to one cosmic plan. At the
restless edge of the city, where the sea-gulls hover motion-
less only to slip gently away, where sun and water give man
the momentary illusion of his coronation by nature, where
boats pass from shore to shore and factory fires flicker, there
one perceives "the simple, compact, well-joined scheme"

and "the certainty of others—the life, love, sight, hearing of others." In that ephemeral instant, Nature touches Civilization through the Individual.

This conjunction of themes so essential to Whitman is effected through an image never directly mentioned but completely present—the island city.* Half-submerged in the poem like Manhattan itself in the bay, the island city is the perfect symbol for a poet celebrating not nature alone, nor the human individual in isolation, but these together in some vital ongoing relationship to society. Leslie Fiedler's shrewd observation that "land is for [Whitman] the island-dweller's land, never removed from the sound of breaking waves or the sight of the mastheads of ships" needs also to have its terms reversed. The sea is for Whitman commonly the city-dweller's sea, seldom removed in the poet's consciousness from the ships—which is to say the society—close at hand. How often we are aware, when the poet stands on the beach alone at night or sees a live-oak growing in Louisiana, of an observer who has come to gaze at nature from some place quite disconnected from nature. Hence a great part of its value to him: it *differs* from the world he knows. Unlike Shelley, Whitman rarely gives us the sense of his standing naked before nature, asking the wind to lift him as a dead leaf, a swift cloud, a panting wave. Unlike the Keats who is moved less by the great untamed outdoors than by pastoral conventions when he asserts,

> To one who has been long in city pent,
> 'Tis very sweet to look into the fair
> And open face of heaven,

* Since writing this essay I have discovered that Leslie Fiedler uses the identical phrase in his excellent compact Introduction to the Dell-Laurel selection of Whitman's poetry (1959). Fiedler emphasizes, though, the island rather than the city. Decidedly an "urban poet," Whitman was, he argues, "even more deeply a poet of beaches and harbors." While I agree with this emphasis, the phrase "urban poet" obscures complexities in Whitman's case that deserve to be explored.

and who reads a book as he "sinks into some pleasant lair/ Of wavy grass" and then returns home in the evening, Whitman often becomes most lyrical when affirming the wonder of man's links to *both* nature and the city. Thus in "Crossing Brooklyn Ferry"—whose very title assumes the double connection—these three themes are continually joined:

> The glories strung like beads on my smallest sights and
>   hearings—on the walk in the street, and the passage
>   over the river,
> The current rushing so swiftly, and swimming with me
>   far away,
> The others that are to follow me, the ties between me
>   and them. . . .
>
> I loved well those cities,
> I loved well the stately and rapid river,
> The men and women I saw were all near to me. . . .
>
> Now I am curious what sight can ever be more stately
>   and admirable to me than my mast-hemm'd Man-
>   hatta,
> My river and sun-set, and my scallop-edged waves of
>   flood-tide,
> The sea-gulls oscillating their bodies, the hay-boat in
>   the twilight, and the belated lighter;
> Curious what Gods can exceed these that clasp me by
>   the hand. . . .

Represented in scrupulous detail, bathed in an amazing poignance, the island city looms in its Manhattan guise most immediately and entirely in "Crossing Brooklyn Ferry." Found here and there throughout the poems, it reappears, sometimes with parallel thematic functions, in the prose. Nature and artifice are joined in such imagery of *Specimen Days* as that in which Whitman writes with obvious wonder and affection of a visit to New York some years after the war.

Sailing north in the bay past Staten Island, with Sandy Hook
and the Atlantic highlands behind, he sees "rising out of
the midst, tall-topt, ship-hemm'd, modern, American, yet
strangely oriental, V-shaped Manhattan, with its compact
mass, its spires, its cloud-touching edifices group'd at the
center—the green of the trees, and all the white, brown and
gray of the architecture well blended, as I see it, under a
miracle of limpid sky, delicious light of heaven above, and
June haze on the surface below." In the passage following
this brilliant image he then states certain political implications of the union of human individuals with the natural and
social spheres:

> Today, I should say—defiant of cynics and pessimists, and
> with a full knowledge of all their exceptions—an appre-
> ciative and perceptive study of the current humanity of
> New York gives the directest proof yet of successful De-
> mocracy, and of the solution of that paradox, the eligi-
> bility of the free and fully developed individual with the
> paramount aggregate.

The "proof" grows, so far as we can tell, out of his experience imaginatively considered:

> In old age, lame and sick, pondering for years on many a
> doubt and danger for this republic of ours—fully aware
> of all that can be said on the other side—I find in this
> visit to New York, and the daily contact and rapport with
> its myriad people, on the scale of the oceans and tides, the
> best, most effective medicine my soul has yet partaken—
> the grandest physical habitat and surroundings of land
> and water the globe affords—namely Manhattan island
> and Brooklyn, which the future shall join in one city—
> city of superb democracy, amid superb surroundings.

Readers of *Democratic Vistas* may recall that Whitman's
contemplation of the same spectacle could also lead him to
quite different conclusions. Reporting there his return to

New York and Brooklyn in September, 1870, again he describes at some length his impressions of the "splendor,
picturesqueness, and oceanic amplitude and rush of these
great cities," saying that his renewed ferry crossings and
hours in Wall Street and elsewhere make him "realize" once
more "that not Nature alone is great in her fields of freedom
and the open air, in her storms . . . the mountains, forests,
sea—but in the artificial, the work of man too is equally
great. . . ." Now, however, he distinguishes between his sen-
sory response to this scene and a more analytical response.
The results are embedded in one of the more emotional portions of this generally agitated essay, climaxed by the famous
series of questions beginning, "Are there, indeed, *men* here
worthy the name?" and closing, "Is there a great moral and
religious civilization—the only justification of a great material one?" These questions, asked of the cities to which
so much of his life and enthusiasm had been given, find an
answer in an image of the metropolis turned desert: "Con-
fess that to severe eyes, using the moral microscope upon humanity, a sort of dry and flat Sahara appears, these cities,
crowded with petty grotesques, malformations, phantoms,
playing meaningless antics." Although his mood could thus
change, the terms in which he understood the political or social question were much the same as those through which the
imagery of his New York poems was sifted. There were the
artifacts and the water and men.

By a kind of imaginative projection, moreover, these
themes coalesce in fictive island cities other than Manhattan
and elsewhere than in mid-nineteenth-century America. At
the time Whitman was completing his first city poems, he
was also developing a sense of the past and future that seriously and interestingly complements his vision of the world
in "Crossing Brooklyn Ferry."

In the mid-1850s, according to Gay Wilson Allen, the
poet grew fascinated with history and ethnology, especially
those of ancient Egypt. In a number of poems written just

before the Civil War he fused this emergent historical sense with his interest in astronomy and his longstanding enthusiasms over the national American destiny. In "Unnamed Lands" (1860), the cities, arts, and nations tens of thousands of years ago are said to "belong to the scheme of the world every bit as much as we now belong to it," even though they have disappeared. The temporal perpetuity of civilization is also a theme in several of the 1860 "Chants Democratic," with cities presented as signs of cultural advance. As time passes, "great cities appear," and they are (for America in this case) one of the principal "glories." Along that painful though certain progress of the United States westward, in which "America illustrates birth, gigantic youth, the promise, the sure fulfilment," the poet can trace the route

> of seeds dropping into the ground—of birth,
> Of the steady concentration of America, inland, upward, to impregnable and swarming places . . . ,
> Of all sloping down there where the fresh free-giver, the mother, the Mississippi flows . . . ,
> Of cities yet unsurveyed and unsuspected. . . .

Despite a certain declamatory and even platitudinous air to many of the verses in which these themes are found, the lines help us appreciate how much clutter often preceded Whitman's abrupt breakthrough to secure poetic statement. This breakthrough did occur, I think, in some of his city poems of the sixties, even though the tide of his creativity was beginning to set against him. Beginning particularly with the chants of the 1860 edition, as R. W. B. Lewis has recently argued, "the intense and personal *self* of Whitman" began its unfortunate metamorphosis into the self-conscious American bard. Essentially right as this argument is, the transformation did not (as Professor Lewis recognizes) in every instance prove destructive.

Whitman's reaching out toward the prophetic and cosmic, however extravagant or absurd it sometimes became, was

after all a natural extension of an imagination, a tempera-
ment, and an idea of the world all inherently expansive. If
the outcome for his poetry could be the sentimental indis-
criminacy of "Pioneers! O Pioneers!," it could also be the
near-excellence of "A Broadway Pageant," a work only
slightly inferior to comparable poems of the first three edi-
tions. In this frequently slighted piece we find Whitman's
distinctive feeling for the sweep of history massively at work
on the Manhattan directly before him. Occasioned by the
New York tour of Japanese envoys and first published in
the New York *Times* for June 1860, "A Broadway Pageant"
deals broadly with America and the Orient. As the following stanzas show, however, these broad themes grow out of
Whitman's excitement over the ritualistic parade:

When million-footed Manhattan, unpent, descends to
its pavements;
When the thunder-cracking guns arouse me with the
proud roar I love;
When the round-mouth'd guns, out of the smoke and
smell I love, spit their salutes;
When the fire-flashing guns have fully alerted me—
when heaven-clouds canopy my city with a delicate
thin haze;
When, gorgeous, the countless straight stems, the
forests at the wharves, thicken with colors;
When every ship, richly drest, carries her flag at the
peak;
When pennants trail, and street-festoons hang from the
windows;
When Broadway is entirely given up to foot-passengers
and foot-standers—when the mass is densest;
When the façades of the houses are alive with people
—when eyes gaze, riveted, tens of thousands at a
time;
When the guests from the islands advance—when the
pageant moves forward, visible;

> When the summons is made—when the answer that
>   waited thousands of years, answers;
> I too, arising, answering, descend to the pavements,
>   merge with the crowd, and gaze with them.

The scene is presented with an extraordinary union of eloquence and precision, so managed as to give the impression
of an observer's active presence, although the observer is not
located physically until the final line. In other respects too
the stanza is something of a poetic performance, with Ho-
meric epithet (*million-footed Manhattan*), varied repetition
(*thunder-cracking guns, round-mouth'd guns, fire-flashing
guns*), subtly emphatic redundancy (*heaven-clouds, foot-
standers*), rhythms as delicate as the cloud-canopy, and a
dozen more intricacies. The metaphorical and syntactical
boldness of line five is, quite simply, awesome.

This spectacle is given for itself and for its historical significance. "Vast desolated cities—the gliding Present—all
of these, and more, are in the pageant-procession." The
envoy-visit is an end and a beginning. Ending is one phase
of history, beginning another. Its original title, "The Errand-
Bearers," reveals better than "A Broadway Pageant" the
theme of national destiny that actually governs the poem. In
the Japanese presence in Manhattan Whitman saw the future opening out: "to us, then, at last, the Orient comes."
As Europe was paying court to America, so now the Far
East too:

> The sign is reversing, the orb is enclosed,
> The ring is circled, the journey is done. . . .

With his now familiar incantation, Whitman looks to the
metamorphosis of an old Asia through the agency of a new,
American civilization:

> I chant the world on my Western Sea;
> I chant, copious, the islands beyond, thick as stars in
>   the sky;

I chant the new empire, grander than any before—As
    in a vision it comes to me;
I chant America, the Mistress—I chant a greater su-
    premacy;
I chant, projected, a thousand blooming cities yet, in
    time, on those groups of sea-islands;
I chant my sail-ships and steam-ships threading the
    archipelagoes. . . .

These thousand Pacific island cities are, we can see, Whitman's Mannahatta lifted, multiplied, and set down on the
mythic passage to India. They are further linked to Mannahatta and the sea, as the Asian and American civilizations
are joined, by an analogous dual image: the ocean-going ships
of men. It was a map of which Whitman became very fond.
He drew and redrew it, most notably in "Song of the Red-
wood-Tree" years later, again with oceans, ships, islands,
and on those thousand islands a thousand cities, peopled
in spirit if not in fact from America.

This map reflects certain contours of Whitman's imagination and certain of its outer limits. The vision of a Manhattan planted on those Pacific islands is, after all, less
imaginative than fanciful. For all the implied dynamism in
the expansion of American empire through time and space,
the elements of this imperial vision are themselves curiously
fixed: Oceans and Islands-Men-Cities; Nature-the Individual-
Civilization. Having early occupied one of the favorite Romantic outposts—at the perimeter of society—Whitman
seems to have found that location agreeable enough to con-
tinue residing there permanently. Although the attitude with
which he regarded the social spectacle shifted from time to
time, the principal imagery through which he perceived that
spectacle remained comparatively stable. While Eliot spoke
with the artist's acute consciousness of his own limits in observing that "every poet's stock of imagery is circumscribed
somewhere," most readers sense in Whitman, despite his
frequently stupefying originality of detail, a certain funda-

mental confinement of view. What we know of his tempera-
ment suggests that behind this limitation there lay a kind
of indolence or lethargy which only an immense bustle
around him or a great torment within could overcome. Out
of the torment could come the Calamus poems; out of the
bustle, his poems of the city.

Apparently Whitman found it difficult, though, simply to
enjoy the metropolitan spectacle in front of him; his delight in the red-and-gold-lettered signs or the thunder-cracking guns is always tinged to a degree by melancholy or offset
by an effort to locate the scene in some historical or other
context. Like a child of Boston rather than Brooklyn, periodically he appears restless in the presence of sensation even
when immersed in the process of anatomizing it. Thus his
recourse to transcendental metaphysics, which often seem
merely an overlay in his poems, or his odd predilection for
discovering an ancestry for New York, even if doing so involved the factitious enterprise of inventing an Indian pedi-
gree for the city by dubbing it "Mannahatta," or his turning,
after the early poems of concrete immediacy, to the study of
the ancient past and the equally remote future, and his insistence that the roots and prospects of the America he knew
were perfectly colossal. Having introduced the city to American poetry, he displayed considerable uncertainty as to what
to do with it.

Beyond the introduction, then, all that he accomplished
was to imbue the city with the interest that springs from
colorful and passionate life, to make his Manhattan an imaginative point of reference for generations of readers and
poets to come, and to force it to live again in a few unfor-
gettable lines.

Babylons Visited

HENRY JAMES

Reviewing *Drum-Taps* unsympathetically in 1865, James observed, "Every tragic event collects about it a number of persons who delight to dwell upon its superficial points—of minds which are bullied by the *accidents* of the affair." The observation may impress us as having been dropped from too lofty a height, especially by one just twenty-two and with only his first story published. But despite his brashness in stating absolutely what art should be, even James the apprentice critic rewards our attention. "The temper of such minds," he continued, "seems to us to be the reverse of the poetic temper; for the poet, although he incidentally masters, grasps, and uses the superficial traits of his theme, is really a poet only in so far as he extracts its latent meaning and holds it up to common eyes." Substituting *novelist* for *poet*, we have James's preferences in the treatment of "tragic events": a desire not to be coerced by the trivial or merely occasional, instead to discover the buried significance and make it public. The preferences might serve as well for great places as for great events, and so they did for James. Looking as he was, at the moment, at such poems as "First O Songs for a Prelude," James could understandably ridicule Whitman's intention "to celebrate the greatness of the city of New York":

Mannahatta a-march—and it's O to sing it well!
It's O for a manly life in the camp.

In time, the ridicule would be further justified by the superiority of James's own celebration, if only in *The Ambassadors,* of the magnificence of Paris. In *that* work of art the writer was not bullied; there he extracted the latent meaning. Had James read "Crossing Brooklyn Ferry" in the 1860 *Leaves of Grass,* though, or read it appreciatively, he might have recognized the very grasp of surfaces and sounding of depths he sought. And when he came in a few short years to feel the enchantment of Continental cities, he might have perceived the kinship he really bore the celebrant of Manhattan. The two writers draw remarkably together in their enormous attraction to the signifying presence of the metropolis. Confronting it, both repeatedly strike notes of wonder, absorption, intensity. The city impresses both of them by its density, and with the possibilities of complication which that density implies. It summons the past for them both, though never so radiantly as it offers them its swarming present.

James's wish to make the larger centers serve artistic ends is evident in his first substantial novel, *Roderick Hudson* (1876). His greatest problems in its composition (as he remembered them afterward for the Preface to the New York edition) were to make Rowland Mallet convincing as the focal consciousness and to set up effective "antitheses" —between Christina Light and Mary Garland, and between a New England village and Rome. Rereading the novel thirty years after its appearance, although he felt a qualified satisfaction with his handling of point of view, he remained dissatisfied with his attempt at the double contrasts of character and place. Christina came to life, he thought, and he implied that Rome did too, but not the provincial American girl or the "small American *ville de province.*"

James's interest in Rowland's consciousness was probably stronger in 1907 than when he wrote the novel. In the book itself his interest seems much more centered on the civilized

atmosphere of a great Italian city and on the crippling impact which that atmosphere could have on a naïve young
American artist. His focus is actually twofold: on cultural
difference and on character change. A defect of the novel is
that these aims are pursued too independently of each other.
That James had thought to link the two is shown by the passage outlining Roderick's first days in Rome:

> . . . the old imperial and papal city altogether delighted
> him; only there he really found what he had been looking
> for from the first, the sufficient negation of his native
> scene. And indeed Rome is the natural home of those
> spirits with which we just now claimed fellowship for
> Roderick—the spirits with a deep relish for the element
> of accumulation in the human picture and for the in-
> finite superpositions of history. It is the immemorial city
> of convention. . . . Roderick's first fortnight was a high
> aesthetic revel. He declared that Rome made him feel and
> understand more things than he could express; he was
> sure that life must have there for all one's senses an in-
> comparable fineness; that more interesting things must
> happen to one there than anywhere else. And he gave
> Rowland to understand that he meant to live freely and
> largely and be as interested as occasion demanded.

Shortly thereafter we learn that Roderick's powers "had thoroughly kindled in the glowing aesthetic atmosphere of
Rome," and later that he found living in Rome (that "in-
comparable sorceress") "was an education to the senses and
the imagination. . . ." But while we can credit Rome with
the youth's change in mood, with "his growing submission
to the mere insidious actual," the really compelling sources
of Roderick's deterioration are not in Rome but in Christina
Light. Love, rather than the foreign city, destroys him.

That result appears, in part, to have been a miscarriage of
purpose, or of purpose too slowly crystallized. James had not

yet completed the novel when its first chapters began to appear in the *Atlantic Monthly,* a circumstance he was to recall as an "embarrassed phase," as "an experience of difficulty and delay," a period of "shy and groping duration." One imbalance in the novel which this delay may help account for is the vitality of Christina, who emerged with "more life than the subject required," and more life also than would allow a rather pallid Mary Garland to hold up her end of the antithesis.

There were other miscalculations. James wanted to *"do"* something magnificent with Rome, for one thing, but the exact nature of that potential magnificence eluded him. Apart from the incompleteness with which he linked Roderick's fate to that city, James found it difficult to name what it was that Rome had evoked for him. The "pictures, ruins, statues, beggars, monks" that Mary sees in Rome are, Rowland tells her, all " 'impregnated with life; they're the results of an immemorial, a complex and accumulated, civilisation.' " The description is not very enlightening. Neither do we learn anything very definite from Rowland's impressions of the Trastevere quarter of Rome as "oppressingly historic . . . weighted with a ponderous past . . . blighted with the melancholy of things that had had their day," or from James's merely literal use of the Colosseum as a trysting place, neglecting that range of religious and historical overtones he was to play upon, however slightly, in "Daisy Miller." James himself felt this thinness in the novel, speaking afterward in the Preface of "the loved Italy" he had tried to represent, lamenting its having been "so much more loved than one has ever been able, even after fifty efforts, to say!" One suspects, particularly in the light of his subsequent novels, that James's comparative failure here stemmed from the rudimentariness of his attempt merely to "surround" his characters "with the appropriate local glow." That conception of his task would not carry him far toward extracting

latent meaning from Rome, which does indeed quite fail
to throb or to reveal any destructive depths behind its attractive surfaces.

Another accident was the New England village, Northampton. "Pathetic" he later called the way in which his repre-
sentational effort "fails of intensity." One reason it failed
(his recollection implies) lay in his conceiving that American village too purely as an idea. He wanted to project, he
said in the Preface, "some more or less vivid antithesis to a
state of civilisation providing for 'art'. . . . What I wanted,
in essence, was the image of some perfectly humane community which was yet all incapable of providing for it"—
and he added, tellingly, "and I had to take what my scant
experience furnished me." Unless he could give the village
real density, however, he could not balance it on the same
scale with Rome, so that Rome missed in that respect also of
making its weight felt. What we glean of Northampton
from the novel is a highly general impression of goodness,
simplicity, and nature.

Indeed we leave Mary Garland, in the closing paragraph,
living with the dead hero's mother "under the New England
elms." That looks like an offhand dab at the picturesque, as
perhaps it partly was; but in sending this virtuous young
creature back to the sheltering canopy of nature James was
obeying an impulse that was soon to find a more developed
expression in his fiction. The place of nature in the world of
artifice became, in fact, an ascendant theme in his next and
much superior novel. *The American* was an attempt, on
Christopher Newman's part and to a degree James's also, to
discover the limits of the city. "Where did urbanity end and
sincerity begin?" Newman wonders of the exquisite Claire,
and the novel as a whole is strongly conceived in just those
terms. Urbanity is the impenetrably "cold, stout, soft, artificial" duchess, the unreachable dowager Marquise de Bellegarde fastened to her dark rooms, but most insistently Urbain, the Marquis de Bellegarde—"a man of forms and

phrases and postures . . . full of possible impertinences and treacheries," possessed of the self-conscious grandeur "of a great façade," and so inflexibly and intolerantly committed to prescribed views as to think it purely a rebuff to Newman's naïveté to say, " 'We all know what Mozart is; our impressions don't date from this evening.' " Sincerity on the other hand is instinct, intuition, spontaneity, light. James not only sets America up against Europe in the novel, cultural innocence against tradition, and all the other oppressively familiar polarities, but also in a special sense the city against nature. The city that signifies thematically in *The American* is really not Paris, as one might suppose, but something else. Paris itself figures remarkably little. The scenes in the Louvre convey historical overtones to American or English readers that similar scenes in, say, the Uffizi galleries at Florence ordinarily would not, and James modestly exploits suggestive local place names, as when he banishes Claire to a convent on the Rue d'Enfer. But the streets, the domestic interiors, the opera, the visible trappings of the aristocracy could for the most part have been duplicated in many cities of Europe. James draws hardly at all upon the uniqueness of Paris, apparently not given pause—as he would be while selecting a locale for *The Ambassadors*—by its legendary character as a city of the senses, the place above all where sight may corrupt, aesthetic delight become ethical dilemma. In an interestingly ambiguous passage the dowager Marquise, speaking to Newman, dissociates herself from the place at large: " 'I can't say I know it. I know my house—I know my friends —I don't know Paris.' " What she *does* know is guile, duplicity, what James nearly always means in the novel by "urbanity." That artifice is the signifying 'city' of *The American.*

The provinces from which "the great Western Barbarian" comes are, of course, a rude San Francisco, young frontier towns, the open American West. If we smile at the statement that "Newman had sat with Western humorists in knots,

round cast-iron stoves" or had "shoveled sand, as a boy, for
supper, and . . . eaten roast dog in a gold-diggers' camp,"
how much more incredible does it seem to have the range of
expression on Claire's face compared in its vastness—even
through Newman's eyes—to "the wind-streaked, cloud-
flecked distance on a Western prairie"! The analogy shows
how exceedingly James wished to link Claire's inherent naturalness to the great American spaces that had helped shape
Newman's own native goodness. Once Claire's reserve begins
to melt under the warmth of Newman's persevering courtship,
he "discovered that she had naturally an abundance of gay-
ety." One of Newman's qualities as a traveler, we learn on
another occasion, is that "he found his way in foreign cities
by divination. . . ." This was one of the tasks James had set
for the Duke of California: to follow his course intuitively,
past arbitrary borders to the truth of things. This course
brings him, with Claire, to the discovery of her innately free
and lively spirit:

> . . . he found himself wondering less every day what
> Madame de Cintré's secrets might be, and more convinced
> that secrets were, in themselves, hateful things to her. She
> was a woman for the light, not for the shade; and her
> natural line was not picturesque reserve and mysterious
> melancholy, but frank, joyous, brilliant action, with just
> so much meditation as was necessary, and not a grain more.
> To this, apparently, he had succeeded in bringing her back.
> He felt, himself, that he was an antidote to oppressive
> secrets; what he offered her was, in fact, above all things a
> vast, sunny immunity from the need of having any.

The passage is not without its ironies, as subsequent events
in the novel would prove, but the revelation is nonetheless
genuine and important.

What it indicates, among other things, is a degree to
which James was now willing to accept nature as a norm. In
Roderick Hudson he had not at bottom accepted it, had in

truth rather patronized it. Mary Garland "had been brought up to think a great deal of 'nature' and nature's innocent laws," we are told near the beginning of her introduction to Rome; "but now Rowland had talked to her ingeniously of the need of man's spirit to refine upon them, her fresh imagination had responded. . . ." She takes notes on culture, in the earnest New England way, but her education is interrupted by the crisis in her relations with Roderick, and his sudden death sends her straight back to the Northampton elms. Had her education not been interrupted, the implication seems clear, Mary could have been coached away from her faith in nature. To rely on nature was itself unnatural, a result of tutoring. Claire's situation in *The American* is much the same, except that as the novel opens she has already been trained away from spontaneity. It is presented as a merit in Newman that he brings her partway back, that he recognizes the genuineness of Valentin, that he detests the affected Urbain. The pathos, irony, realism, and even comedy of the novel lie partially in Newman's inability to return Claire far enough to natural conduct. He discovers to his pleasure that artifice has its limits—but also, to his chagrin, that nature has limits which artifice defines. It is a discovery about the city that Dreiser's pagans will make at much simpler and more primitive levels of conduct, and with far less capacity than Newman has for stoical resignation.

The city theme principally developed in *The American* thus depends rather tangentially on specific place; the historical Paris and the city of artifice are comparatively disjunct. In this respect the novel does resemble *Roderick Hudson:* the significant action unfolds more or less independently of locale. This relative dissociation of action from setting causes no particular difficulties in *The American,* because (as the Preface intimates) James had not set out, as he had in the earlier book, to connect them tightly, and the finished work does not perceptibly suffer from his not

having done so. The point is germane to our appreciation
of James's handling of city-place. Alive as he was to the
fascination of European cities, pre-eminently so among Americans abroad, his use of them for his art was selective in the
extreme. From the *Transatlantic Sketches* of 1875 through
the *Italian Hours* of 1909, his copious travel essays reveal
how unreservedly he could enjoy large and small towns
throughout England, France, and Italy. The fervor some of
them aroused in him, particularly Paris and a few choice
Italian cities, is seen in his ecstatic letter to William when
he first visited Rome in 1869: "At last—for the first time
—I live! It beats everything: it leaves the Rome of your
fancy—your education—nowhere. . . . I went reeling and
moaning thro' the streets, in a fever of enjoyment. . . ." But
in his fiction, nearly everywhere, he had this fever very much
under control. His novels and tales of the city divide with
considerable distinctness into those in which city-place is
treated simply, prosaically, and tonelessly, and those in which
it carries part of the burden of meaning through suggestive-
ness. To the first group, as I have indicated, belongs *The
American;* to the latter, at least by intention, *Roderick
Hudson.*

This division into prosaic and poetic cities corresponds,
on its negative side, to the basic 'international' contrast. The
expressive cities of James's fiction are always European, never
American. Nowhere in *The Europeans, Washington Square,
The Bostonians,* the *Tales of Three Cities* or other stories
with American settings does urban place function so evoc-
atively as in the well-known passage in *The American
Scene* where the sixty-year-old expatriate describes his "fine
exhilaration" at the sight of New York harbor.* And even

* By limiting my comment in this chapter largely to James's handling of city-*place,* I do not intend to minimize the interest or impor-
tance of other aspects of the city in his work. From the James canon
one necessarily selects, always with an enormous sense of things
omitted. Other studies might well take up the peculiarly urban idea
of artifice represented in *The American,* with its variant in *The Euro-*

in that sensitive account of his return—remarkable for its parallels to Whitman's description in *Democratic Vistas* of his own home-coming up the Bay some thirty years before —James finds the "commanding and thrilling" elements of the scene counterbalanced by his impressions of an urban technology radically menacing in its power, suggestive for the future of "some colossal set of clockworks, some steel-souled machine-room of brandished arms and hammering fists and opening and closing jaws." New York and Boston were quite different quantities to him throughout his life— a difference he plays upon in a minor way in the divergent characters of Milly Theale and Susan Stringham in *The Wings of the Dove*—but they were alike in failing to lift the dampness of spirit that settled on James in the American environment. In the cities of Europe he could "live!"— which meant to enjoy, but also to be responsive, stirred, struck by their possibilities for fiction.

Following *Roderick Hudson*, this responsiveness to place showed itself again most notably in *The Portrait of a Lady*. For Isabel Archer, the Italian cities do not just provide "atmosphere," though they do that, nor do they appear as deeply affecting her, in the way they were supposed to have affected the young sculptor of the earlier novel. Instead, they *signify* —first of all through the attachments James establishes of character to place. One of the first remarks Mrs. Touchett makes to Isabel after their meeting in Albany is that " 'You should go to Florence if you like houses in which things have happened—especially deaths' "; and we are reminded peri-

---

peans, which sets the foreign city in a special and complicated fashion down on an American landscape owing much less to the Boston countryside it purports to be than to certain conventions of pastoral comedy. Or one might examine how dependent the social drama of *Washington Square, The Bostonians, The Princess Casamassima,* or *The Tragic Muse* actually is on the metropolitan milieu of each, or —in a comparable but narrower inquiry—how integral specifically urban detail is to such stories as "An International Episode," "In the Cage," or "The Beast in the Jungle," or to such longer works as *The Aspern Papers* and *The Wings of the Dove.*

odically in this novel of marriages that one of the "irregular" features of Mrs. Touchett's marriage, one of the "unnatural things" less purely comic than grotesque, is her living apart from her husband eleven months of the year, he in England, she in Florence. (Mr. Touchett is confined to a mechanical chair, but that fact lacks the definite sexual import it has for Clifford Chatterley in the Lawrence novel.) Associated distinctly with Florence also is Madame Merle, whose coldness, unlike Mrs. Touchett's, is serious and exploitative. When at last she makes her delayed appearance in the novel, she introduces herself to Isabel by saying, " 'I'm an old friend of your aunt's. I've lived much in Florence. I'm Madame Merle.' " And when in turn the name of Gilbert Osmond is first mentioned, of course by Madame Merle, he is emphatically and almost exclusively identified with Italy: " 'He's Gilbert Osmond—he lives in Italy; that's all one can say about him or make of him.' " Shortly thereafter she reveals Osmond's whereabouts as Florence, and it is at his villa there that he is presented to the reader, and inside Mrs. Touchett's palace in Florence, to Isabel.

Making her initial visit to Osmond (driving out of the city through the Roman gate), Isabel wonders aloud, after she has talked with him for a while, whether " 'I should forsake my natural mission if I were to settle in Florence.' " She is forced to forsake it, as we know, although the place where she settles, with Osmond, is Rome. That more monstrous city farther south really proves but the culmination of what had commenced at Florence. With its "deep appeal" for Isabel, the Rome that gave her the happiest days of her life during Osmond's courtship shows quite another face after her marriage. (The reader, though not Isabel, can detect sinister implications in that suitor's "correct and ingenious" little sonnet, "Rome Revisited.") Almost as soon as we learn of the marriage, the Osmond palace is described in such a way as to suggest how Isabel's freedom has been destroyed, how the immense Rome of the days of her "felicity" has shrunk to the confines of a single house and turned malign. The description of the Palazzo Roccanera comes to us through the eyes of Pansy's suitor, but it speaks mainly of Isabel's new life:

> The object of Mr. Rosier's well-regulated affection dwelt in a high house in the very heart of Rome; a dark and massive structure overlooking a sunny *piazzetta* in the neighbourhood of the Farnese Palace. In a palace, too, little Pansy lived—a palace by Roman measure, but a dungeon to poor Rosier's apprehensive mind. It seemed to him of evil omen that the young lady he wished to marry, and whose fastidious father he doubted of his ability to conciliate, should be immured in a kind of domestic fortress, a pile which bore a stern old Roman name, which smelt of historic deeds, of crime and craft and violence, which was mentioned in "Murray" and visited by tourists who looked, on a vague survey, disappointed and depressed, and which had frescoes by Caravaggio in the *piano nobile* and a row of mutilated statues and dusty urns in the wide, nobly-arched loggia overhanging the damp court where a fountain gushed out of a mossy niche.

Thus immured, Isabel has exchanged her natural mission—which was the mission to be natural—for Osmond's unnatural one, her wings for his antique medallions. She has met circumstance, has had to surrender, in a word, to fate.

On that momentous afternoon when Madame Merle cruelly reveals that she has had "Everything!" to do with Isabel's marriage, the girl's first act is to drive past the Roman walls out into the country. There, walking over the fields and flowers, she thinks of how her life has become intermingled with that ancient city. "She had become deeply, tenderly acquainted with Rome; it interfused and moderated her passion. But she had grown to think of it chiefly as the place where people had suffered." It is as a place where she too must inescapably suffer that Isabel comes to think of that city of martyrs. Once she learns the full truth about Osmond and returns temporarily to the Touchett home in England, "she thought with a kind of spiritual shudder of Rome." Her thoughts are at the same moment of Osmond, and of her ruined life. "There was a penetrating chill in the image," James says of the city whose ruins had merely made her own "catastrophe" seem "less unnatural"; "and she drew back into the deepest shade of Gardencourt." It was Gardencourt, indeed, that "had been her starting-point," she reflects in these concluding English hours, and which she had recalled in her unhappy days at Rome as holding "something sacred." Gardencourt—nature tamed but cultivated— seems her proper "sanctuary," but she returns at the end to Rome. She has promised not to desert Pansy, she feels that life may revive for her, she thinks of her marital obligations, she flees from an aggressive Caspar Goodwood—these motives appear but do not wholly account for her return. This final journey is in part symbolic, as her earliest descent to the cities of the south had been. Now Isabel accepts Rome, which is to say, her fate: the inevitability of complication, limitation, suffering.

In *The Ambassadors,* some twenty years later, James again sends his protagonist through the symbolic journey into the city; but the nature of that journey, of a piece with other permutations distinguishing his later from his earlier work, has changed. Once more the city represents a kind of destiny for the hero, attracting and then enclosing, associated by implication with both his singular fate and that of mankind generally. But in *The Ambassadors* that fate has become less social and more inward, less a termination and more a development, no less complicating and restricting but distinctly more benign. The various cities of *The Portrait of a Lady* have now been reduced essentially to one city; the hero's progress is now not so much toward the city as into and

through it. The city is not so nearly a pole of experience as
it is coterminous with experience.

Quickly after Strether's arrival there, Paris, the overwhelmingly *present* city of his destination, becomes for him
a gliding wonder. It is Spring when he arrives, and though
he is already thinking in the first moments that he has, "as
he had often privately expressed it, Paris to reckon with,"
his simple arithmetical correctness faces sooner than he could
have anticipated the Parisian sensuousness that initially de-
lights and then bewilders him. He lingers first and most
attentively in the Tuileries and the Luxembourg gardens,
where he becomes dimly conscious of the interplay of nature
with art that pleases and confuses him to the end. On a
succeeding day "the sharp spell of Paris" seizes him, and
from then until he declares in one of his parting observations to Maria Gostrey regarding his European venture that
" 'Of course I moved among miracles,' " Strether advances
toward the center of truths continually intimated and made
manifest by that miraculous city.

Its magic transcends his momentary appreciations; Paris
affects him. Standing on the street opposite Chad's apartment, the earnest missionary finds himself confronting an
experience nothing had quite prepared him for. "Poor
Strether had at this very moment to recognize the truth
that, wherever one paused in Paris, the imagination, before
one could stop it, reacted." The most remarkable instance of
this involuntary response occurs a bit earlier in the novel,
while he is seated in the Luxembourg gardens. "His greatest
uneasiness seemed to peep at him out of the possible impression that almost any acceptance of Paris might give one's
authority away."

It hung before him this morning, the vast bright Babylon,
like some huge iridescent object, a jewel brilliant and
hard, in which parts were not to be discriminated nor

differences comfortably marked. It twinkled and trembled and melted together, and what seemed surface one moment seemed all depth the next.

This luminous vision perfectly projects Strether's mind at the outset of his education—with his anxious scruples, his predilection for giving moral symbols priority over facts, his fastidious interest in sin, his tidy conception of moral distinctions, his fear of failure through falling. In short, it mirrors the Woollett in him—the New England town which, like its chief resident, Mrs. Newsome, appears in the novel only as a state of mind. Perceiving Paris as Babylon is itself the act of an intellect accustomed to the vague and faintly secular Biblicality of nineteenth-century New England. The Paris that Strether actually encounters, by contrast, is substantial, immediate, and stubbornly mystifying. At the same time, the vividness of his glimpse of Babylon suggests that Strether *has* an imagination, and that he can therefore—unlike Jim and Sarah Pocock—ultimately respond to the complexities which Paris thrusts before him.

Much turns in the novel on his responsiveness to the singular appeal of Paris—in a way, everything does. His first reflection after the iridescent Babylon appears to him is that "it was a place of which, unmistakably, Chad was fond; wherefore, if he, Strether, should like it too much, what on earth, with such a bond, would become of either of them?" A moment after, he raises the question that defines the nature of his enterprise as a whole: "Was it at all possible . . . to like Paris enough without liking it too much?" The novel answers that question in a variety of ways, but for Strether the critical answer is No. By the time Mrs. Newsome has dispatched her other ambassadors abroad, he admits in an exchange with Jim Pocock to having " 'liked my Paris . . . too much,' " by which is meant, in part, that he has come to appreciate its complexities—that is, the complexities of human conduct there, and so everywhere—and that this knowledge spells for him a kind of fatality.

The extraordinary intimacy with which his life is involved with the city is shown partly through contrasts with the chief minor characters. Little Bilham is one with the older man in his susceptibility to place but has allowed it, as his friend has not, to overcome his power to act. "He had come out to Paris to paint—to fathom, that is, at large, that mystery; but study had been fatal to him so far as anything *could* be fatal, and his productive power faltered in proportion as his knowledge grew." Two or three pages of the encounter between the elder Pococks and the emerging allies Strether and Marie de Vionnet are given over to the grimly humorous nuances of Sarah's smug remark, " 'I *know* Paris,' " to which Mme. de Vionnet replies after a time that " 'It's he [Strether], I gather, who has learned to know his Paris. . . .' " Of course, Chad and Maria Gostrey have preceded and in important respects paralleled Strether in their liking and knowing. Chad differs from the hero principally in the greater ease with which he settled into Mme. de Vionnet's city and the greater facility with which, it seems at the end, he is about to leave it. Miss Gostrey differs from Strether mainly in the degree of her involvement; she serves after all chiefly as an accessory to what her friend describes to her one day as " 'the fate that waits for one, the dark doom that rides.' "

In this expression Strether melodramatizes a little, aware —"with his fairly open sense of the irony of things"—that he does so. But the intuition that Paris is somehow to frame his destiny has occurred to him seriously on that initiatory Spring morning (when he wonders about "the fate [which was] decreed for him") and stays with him until he recognizes its truth. When he breakfasts with Bilham and Waymarsh in Chad's apartment, "with the great hum of Paris coming up in softness, vagueness—for Strether himself indeed already positive sweetness—" he felt "a precipitation in his fate." During his romantic *déjeûner* with Mme. de Vionnet near the Seine, on the Left Bank, after their accidental meeting in Notre Dame, the American realizes how firmly he has moved over to her side—and also how little he has controlled that choice.

> The sense that he had had before, the sense he had had repeatedly, the sense that the situation was running away with him, had never been so sharp as now. . . . What had come over him as he recognized her in the nave of the church was that holding off could be but a losing game from the instant she was worked for not only by her subtlety, but by the hand of fate itself. If all the accidents were to fight on her side—and by the actual showing they loomed large—he could only give himself up. This was what he had done in privately deciding then and there to propose she should breakfast with him. What did the success of his proposal in fact resemble but the smash in which a regular runaway properly ends? The smash was their walk, their *déjeûner,* their omelette, the Chablis, the place, the view, their present talk and his present pleasure in it. . . .

After his further tacit commitment to Marie in the presence of the Pococks, "his position [had] grown to affect him as quite excitingly, altogether richly, inevitable"; and in their poignant farewell at the end of everything, Marie shows, in remarking to Strether on the outcome of her life, that while the inevitable can be melancholy as well as exciting, it is in any event what one must accept: " 'It's a doom—I know it; you can't see it more than I do myself. Things have to happen as they will.' " In this, as in so much else, she speaks with the voice of Paris.

That the American's doom has also proved a kind of salvation is but one of the multiple ironies generated by "that great ironic city." "The immeasurable town" that Strether had distinctly felt in Gloriani's garden "sweeping away, as by a last brave brush, his usual landmarks and terms" has not so much given him new landmarks and terms as it has overwhelmed him with the force of life, or rather of 'living,' of beauty, of the inexplicable. Paris has proved destructive, in some ways as Rome was supposed to prove for Roderick Hudson and in other ways for Isabel, but it has destroyed mainly Strether's reluctance to "live." By the time it has destroyed his innocence also, learning as he finally does the truth about Chad's relations with Mme. de Vionnet, he has already committed himself to the virtues it embodies, too late to turn back had he wanted to. But he shows no signs of wanting to; his commitment has been made to "pagan" life—James's word, oft-repeated, as it will be Dreiser's—and no one displays that life in the novel half so beautifully as the urbane couple whose outing in the country he interrupts. In the scene where their boat enters his field of vision, his painter's "frame," nature and artifice are infinitely confused. The question Newman raised in his own mind of Claire—"Where did urbanity end and sincerity begin?"—here receives a more distinct answer than in that earlier novel. They can be, and ideally are, inextricable. Of this large human possibility James's city becomes, at the end, the elaborate and simple emblem.

Landscape of Hysteria

STEPHEN CRANE

So accustomed are we to pigeonholing Stephen Crane as a war novelist and a naturalistic novelist that the distinctive character of his city fiction has not been plainly identified. The practice has been to refer to his city writings obliquely, to the extent that they mirror preoccupations of the French naturalists. But the city Crane envisioned has its own fascinations and, like so much else that this precocious child of Newark, New Jersey, wrote about in his telescoped lifetime, a considerable originality.

His first long tale, *Maggie,* published in 1893, remains in one's mind as primitively simple. The tone is objective, the plot line elementary, the characters sketched, the dialogue compact and direct, all resources economized. Howells' commendatory term for it was "Greek." Yet this novella overflows with the city ruck. Occupations abound. The leading characters include a wage-worker (job unspecified), a beggar, a bartender, a truck-driver, a police-blotter drunk (Maggie's mother), and a female operative in a small collar-and-cuff sweatshop (Maggie), later a prostitute. Glimpsed are dock-workers, a tugboat engineer, prison convicts, mission preachers, soupline-ticket seekers, the cops, streetcar and fire-engine drivers, pedestrians, beer-hall musicians, waiters, table girls, dancers, singers, comedians and a ventriloquist, *bier*-swilling Germans and sailors, a bouncer, flower-dealers, and upper-crust theater-goers.

Because Crane reputedly wrote the first draft of this story in a fraternity house at Syracuse University and only afterward got to know New York City slum life well, many of these local particulars must have been inserted in revisions. However it came about, the twenty-one-year-old author showed an uncanny gift for selecting *highly* relevant detail. In *Maggie,* Crane provokes little of the feeling one gets from Howells' *A Modern Instance* or Melville's *Pierre* that the urban circumstances are often arbitrary, that most of the narrative could have been laid anywhere. The vocations of Crane's Bowery characters seem most appropriate to the Bowery, and the same holds for the frenetic tempo he sets for their forced lives. There are street-gang brawls, street-corner lounging, and fire-engine clamor; indoors there is saloon life, beer-hall life, popular melodrama. An Italian is a victim of petty theft, a Chinaman of assault, a "dago" embattled. Centrally, there is the society of fire-escapes, clutter, families, uproar, cooking odors, boozing, ruined maidens, and that general proximity to the "gutter" (Crane's word) peculiar to city tenements.

In spite of a youthful simplicity and a certain allegorical crudity about the whole, *Maggie* is superior to Howells' novel of three years before, *A Hazard of New Fortunes,* partly because Crane was willing to consider the lower classes real. The opportunities for Howells had been immense. There was novelty of subject in the immigrants' New York of the 1880s, there was the impetus of his lingering outrage over the Haymarket executions, the stimulation for himself and his readers of recurrent social crises in the major cities, the chance to make literary use of Americans' growing consciousness of the city as a distinct form of experience and of country-dwellers as curious, unenlightened types. For this novel, moreover, Howells had had the inspiration of

making his hero, Basil March, a peculiarly urban kind of
provincial who, secure in the bourgeois privacies of job and
home, suddenly removes himself in middle age to the dis-
quietudes of a greater city. It was an astute idea, of a piece
with Christopher Newman's (and later Lambert Strether's)
journey to Paris, foreshadowing Hurstwood's removal to
New York, preparing us for the ingenious variation of
Henderson's trek to become a rain king in an African village.

But Howells could not bring it off. He recognized how
necessary it was for his hero to blossom under the New
York sun. He asserts that his hero does blossom: earlier,
Basil March had regarded life there as a "spectacle," but
now "a sense of the striving and the suffering deeply possessed him. . . ." Howells failed, however, to demonstrate
this evolution in Basil's feelings. In the latter half of the
novel Basil acts pretty much as he did before, though his
pensiveness takes on a more melancholy hue following the
deaths of Conrad Dryfoos and Lindau. On his way home
through a street-car strike—he rides, imperturbably, with
the scabs—he has just witnessed Lindau fatally clubbed by
a policeman and found Conrad shot dead. These killings
move him only to a temporary sadness and to half-hearted
meditations. But if Basil's encounters with the destructive
realities of the city are to *mean* anything, it is essential that
he be shocked, or at least interpret the killings seriously.
Neither happens. Basil refrains, he draws back from the
experience.

In the end, therefore, Howells' city remains unfathomed.
The street-car workers, the drunk in the gutter, the Spaniards
who run the restaurants, the Negro janitors, the eyes and
earrings of Italians that "twinkled in and out of the alley-
ways and basements" all remain for the Marches what they
were in the beginning—*picturesque*. They are, to use Howells' vocabulary, not real, both because they are not ordinary
enough and because they are too ordinary. He knew from
experience that pleasant middle-class life was real; but out

of a mingled caution, ignorance, incuriosity, and dislike, he could not bring himself to believe that the inferior social orders were also real, that there *were* lower depths. One result was that Howells could not assess even middle-class life in any but the shallowest terms, from the inside.

Although he wrote from a vantage-point outside the center of lower-class experience too, Crane assumed that there was a center and tried to imagine what it was like. This effort is, I think, one element in what critics have often spoken of as his modernity. Other, more purely aesthetic elements in this modernity have been analyzed discerningly by John Berryman, its philosophic elements with equal discernment by Richard Chase. But beyond even the special proletarian, ironic, and amoral quantities he brought into American fiction, Crane introduced something more. The nature of that further quantity is suggested by certain singularities of perception in his city stories.

Now and again in *Maggie* he pauses, or his characters pause, to peer, up or down or across, from, into, or along some vista made possible by the sheer physical actuality of the city. In the opening scene, as small boys scuffle wildly at a gravel heap, "dodging, hurling stones, and swearing in barbaric trebles,"

> from a window of an apartment-house that uprose from amid squat ignorant stables there leaned a curious woman. Some laborers, unloading a scow at a dock at the river, paused for a moment and regarded the fight. The engineer of a passive tugboat hung lazily over a railing and watched.

Another time, Maggie's brother Jimmie and a neighbor woman stand together in the hall of their tenement, listening:

> Above the muffled roar of conversation, the dismal wailings of babies at night, the thumping of feet in unseen corridors and rooms, and the sound of varied hoarse

shoutings in the street and the rattling of wheels over cobbles, they heard the screams of the child and the roars of the mother die away to a feeble moaning and a subdued bass muttering.

Elsewhere, sweating away in her collar-and-cuff shop, Maggie "knew she was gradually and surely shrivelling in the hot, stuffy room. The begrimed windows rattled incessantly from the passing of elevated trains. The place was filled with a whirl of noises and odors." And so on.

In these passages that now seem almost contrived for the movie-maker's art, there is more than an ordinary apprehension of city space, smell, and sound. In most such passages in *Maggie,* and again in his other Bowery fiction, *George's Mother* (written 1893–94 and published 1896), the angle of perception seems familiar but rather dislocated—as though something in the experience or the observer or one acting on the other had displaced a normal perspective. This strangeness is more apparent in a longer excerpt, here from Chapter II where Jimmie and his father trudge home:

> Eventually they entered a dark region where, from a careening building, a dozen gruesome doorways gave up loads of babies to the street and the gutter. A wind of early autumn raised yellow dust from cobbles and swirled it against a hundred windows. Long streamers of garments fluttered from fire-escapes. In all unhandy places there were buckets, brooms, rags, and bottles. In the street infants played or fought with other infants or sat stupidly in the way of vehicles. Formidable women, with uncombed hair and disordered dress, gossiped while leaning on railings, or screamed in frantic quarrels. Withered persons, in curious postures of submission to something, sat smoking pipes in obscure corners. A thousand odors of cooking food came forth to the street. The building quivered and creaked from the weight of humanity stamping about in its bowels.

The manner is ordinary, yet extra-ordinary. *Careening building, infants . . . fought . . . or sat stupidly, Withered persons, in curious postures of submission,* and the whole last sentence—these details yoke realistic surface to a deeply non-realistic way of perceiving that surface. It is as though what others accept as normal Crane sees as tortured; or as though he detects what is fantastic in the accustomed.

Those tales in which Crane's sense of disordered experience appears most acute are, with one or two exceptions, of war and the city. This sense is most pronounced in *The Red Badge of Courage* and such battle pieces as "An Episode of War," and in *Maggie* and *George's Mother.* There is evidence of it also in two competent short works of fictionalized reporting, "The Men in the Storm" and "An Experiment in Misery," whose otherwise neutral tone and surface rendering of hunger and poverty on the flophouse circuit in New York remind one of Orwell's Paris and London reminiscences forty years later. Quickly in his writing apprenticeship, Crane's special talent gravitated to the two major subjects that have ever since seemed uncommonly well suited to it. That he lacked first-hand acquaintance with battles before writing *The Red Badge of Courage* or prolonged contact with the lower East Side before his New York stories, yet represented both so convincingly, suggests how indebted he was to an existing body of notions and impressions of war and the city. Eccentric as his vision was, nevertheless it appears to have expressed marvelously certain feelings of disorientation men have had in the face of those vast social instruments of unseen powers, from his father's generation down through ours. The respect with which *Red Badge* has been received over the years right from the moment of its appearance, in spite of stylistic and other ineptitudes that would sink less gifted writers, appears to justify Hemingway's praise of the story as "that great boy's dream of war that was to be truer to how war is than any war the boy who wrote it would ever live to see." Hemingway's affection for a prose and a career so like his own prompts us to discount slightly his eulogies of *Red Badge*, just as critics have discounted Howells' admiration for *Maggie* because its realistic features exemplified his literary doctrines. Of course we should make both discounts, admitting at the same time that we have in Hemingway and Howells unusually qualified witnesses.

The power that these two and many other have felt in Crane's vision of war and the city may be described by saying that for him these were not solely arenas of experience, they were *kinds* of experience. Along the short band of experience to which Crane was tuned, modern warfare and city life reverberated together. Coercive, too huge for any one individual to comprehend, violent or conducive to violence, promoting friction between individuals or between old and new patterns of conduct, indifferent to results, both war and the city have as we know bred feelings of strangeness, unease, betrayal, fear, dislocation. But they have bred excitement, release, expectation, and wonder too, as the responses of Whitman alone prove. It was Crane's role to testify to dislocation, to that condition of modern life in which persons are found "in curious postures of submission to something."

Indeed their "postures" interested him very much. If we turn back for a moment to a more general view of his fiction, we can see more clearly how that is so. To begin with, Crane seems little concerned with place. As in most American fiction, the lone human figure commands his attention, and the fact that he writes again and again of nearly the same enraged, anxious man strengthens our impression of Crane as preoccupied by character. When we examine what it is about Henry Fleming or Jimmie or George that he touches upon, however, we find that he cares little about their history prior to the story itself, and inside the story makes little effort to re-create the intricacies of relations between human individuals. The dynamics of psychology quite eluded him.

While the minds of his principal characters are somewhat complex, they are also relatively inert. Even when he wants one of them to develop, as he did most evidently in *Red Badge* but also in *Maggie* and *George's Mother,* he is noticeably inept at dramatizing any change. Particularly in the light of his bewitchment with the psyche, these clinical deficiencies may surprise us.

What *does* intrigue Crane is the posture, the act of perceiving, the peering out. His awareness of the phenomenon of awareness, though far more rudimentary than James's, is no less intense. Its force springs partly from an uncommon directness of relationship between perceiver and environment. Awareness is not turned in upon itself through memory or elaborate ruminations or the unfolding of associated images; it is turned straight outward upon objects perceived simply but with an unusual sensitivity. Though *George's Mother* is generally more restrained than the preceding slum tale, it too conveys this luminous intensity.

She looked out at chimneys growing thickly on the roofs. A man at work on one seemed like a bee. In the intricate yards below, vine-like lines had strange leaves of cloth. To her ears there came the howl of the man with the red, mottled face. He was engaged in a furious altercation with the youth who had called attention to his poor aim. They were like animals in a jungle.

In the distance an enormous brewery towered over the other buildings. Great gilt letters advertised a brand of beer. Thick smoke came from funnels and spread near it like vast and powerful wings. The structure seemed a great bird, flying. The letters of the sign made a chain of gold hanging from its neck. The little old woman looked at the brewery. It vaguely interested her, for a moment, as a stupendous affair, a machine of mighty strength.

Presently she sprang from her rest and began to buffet

with her shrivelled arms. . . . Terrific blows were given
and received.

Whether battling the dust and dirt in her apartment, which
is all the little old woman actually does in the chapter from
which this fragment is taken, or peering out and down from
her window, this character is curiously responsive to her
surroundings. She detects chimneys growing, laundry as
strange leaves on vines, a brewery as a monstrous bird and
then a machine, grime as an enemy.

The strangeness in the world about her is also her strangeness. Because it remains ambiguous in the excerpt above, as
in much of the story, whether the perceiving mind is the
character's or Crane's, we cannot say certainly that the queerness exists only in her mind or only in her surroundings. For
Crane it seems present in both, almost indistinguishably. One
dissonance sounds for the other.

It is not so much character or environment, then, to which
Crane addresses himself as it is a relationship between a
particular sort of character and a particular sort of environment, a peculiar emotionalism in certain egos and a singular
disorder in the military or urban worlds to which those
egos submit. Of numerous commentators on this difficult
writer, only Charles C. Walcutt (in *American Literary Naturalism*) has made an effort to decipher this relationship.
Although his key is literary naturalism, Walcutt has read
Crane with his own good eyes, and one result is to put
some of the stories into a context other than naturalism and
in major respects more illuminating. Almost as an afterthought, Walcutt mentions how closely Crane's work resembles some plays (nearly all of a later date) by Strindberg,
Kaiser, Kaufman, and O'Neill. He finds in both expres-
sionistic drama and Crane's prose "a sense of outrage, of
hysterical folly, of a reality so wrenched that it appears hal-
lucinatory." Walcutt's detailed commentaries on the longer
tales support this observation. The illusions of the unheroic

hero in *Red Badge* mirror "the insanely grotesque and incongruous world of battle into which he is plunged," and in *Maggie* there is a similar "landscape of hysteria"—a phrase that suggests beautifully Crane's matching of irrationalities in person and place. This correspondence is strongly established in these stories of war and the city, one should add, but not in "The Blue Hotel" (as Walcutt's analysis silently reveals) or in "The Monster," where it is missing altogether.

Presented less extremely and less consistently than in *Maggie,* the sense of disorientation is nevertheless marked in *George's Mother.* In a way, the enormous brewery the woman spies from her window towers over the whole story. In its most vivid scene, her son, George, gets blindingly drunk, and sights and sounds about him in a friend's apartment come and go through his increasingly unfocused senses. His abnormal perception in this scene differs only in mode and degree from that which his mother experienced at the window. Both deviations flow out of the special circumstances of city life. When George arrived in New York from an outlying town (perhaps a village), he found it "an impenetrable mystery." He comes to believe that to know the city one must undergo the unsettling sensations of heavy drinking. (Before long, Crane tells us, he could drink ten to twenty beers—without shivering.) "When he knew its saloons he comprehended the street." But the alcohol throws his life into further disorder. He never does find his way in the city, nor does his mother, who presumably also grew up in the country, whose tract-toting, temperance-loving, house-tidying habits appear inappropriate in her new surroundings, and the cause of whose death is vaguely linked with her son's errant ways there.

If in the naturalism of "The Open Boat" Crane reminds us of no one so perfectly as Hemingway, his expressionism may well call to mind a near-contemporary, Kafka. The vocabulary of painting can mislead when applied to literature, working as it does through broader analogy than most literary criticism, but it can sometimes reveal when other means fail. Walcutt realized its applicability to Crane, naming modern painters with whom the novelist might be compared: Cézanne, Matisse, van Gogh. Although Walcutt lumps the three together, rather unfortunately, as "impressionists," and might have strengthened his point by mentioning only van Gogh and (say) Edvard Munch and the later Emil Nolde, the parallel is sound. On the other hand, a comparison of Crane with Kafka in similar terms may serve to place the contours of Crane's imagination in still clearer relief.

The initial tenement-district scene in *The Trial* finds Joseph K. (*en route* to his first interrogation) pausing and observing much as Crane's characters are wont to do:

> In one corner of the courtyard a line was stretched between two windows, where washing was already being hung up to dry. A man stood below superintending the work with an occasional shout.
>
> K. turned toward the stairs to make his way up to the Court of Inquiry, but then came to a standstill again, for in addition to this staircase he could see in the courtyard three other flights of stairs and besides these a little passage at the other end which seemed to lead into a second courtyard. He was annoyed that he had not been given more definite information about the room, these people showed a strange negligence or indifference in their treatment of him, he intended to tell them so very positively and clearly. Finally, however, he climbed the first stairs and his mind played in retrospect with the saying of the warder Willem that an attraction existed between the Law and guilt, from which it should really follow that the Court of Inquiry must abut on the particular flight of stairs which K. happened to choose.
>
> On his way up he disturbed many children who were

playing on the stairs and looked at him angrily as he
strode through their ranks. "If I ever come here again,"
he told himself, "I must either bring sweets to cajole
them with or else a stick to beat them." Just before he
reached the first floor he had actually to wait for a moment
until a marble came to rest, two children with the lined,
pinched faces of adult rogues holding him meanwhile
by his trousers; if he had shaken them off he must have
hurt them, and he feared their outcries.

Even in so brief a passage we discover notable similarities
to Crane's city fiction—the mixture of realistically observed
detail and a puzzling use of that detail, the character's mingled submissiveness and hostility.

Where Crane's characters relate to each other on a plausi-
bly everyday plane, however, even if not intricately, Kafka's
rarely communicate at all, and whatever contact they do
establish is unexpected, capricious, or otherwise abnormal.
(Why do the children detain K.? Why do their faces seem
threatening? And why does he fear their outcries?) This
sense of disconnectedness extends, in Kafka, to relationships
between characters and their environment, as in K.'s lack
of surprise (elsewhere in the chapter) at the warehouse
function or peculiar interior design of the building where
he is to be questioned. All these improbabilities belong, of
course, to the fantasy world of dream, in which connections
are largely implicit and symbolic. Crane's focus, by contrast,
is on the *connectedness* of his characters with experience
outside themselves. For him, despite the immensity and im-
personality of war or the city, the objective world is knitted
to the subjective, is in a way its expression. Joseph K. sees
only a clothes-line, where washing is hung up to dry; but
George's mother sees "vine-like lines" with "strange leaves
of cloth."

Kafka's universe is, in a word, surrealist, best interpreted
in sexual or political or religious terms deriving partly from

outside the fable itself. Crane's expressionism is simpler and more direct; its outrageous colors do not solicit interpretation of the author's meaning, they summon us to appreciate his mood. Both imaginations belong unmistakably to contemporary urban life, whose creatures they show themselves to be by the barely repressed violence through which they represent that life.

Heathen Catacombs

THEODORE DREISER

James had the gift, rare for a novelist, of poetic compression, so that even his briefer sentences can bare his sensibility as a whole. For all their differences, Crane's talent was also distinctly compressive and figurative. Dreiser's deepest impulses were to *explain*. Loose, expansive, discursive, his prose dips haphazardly into metaphor then suddenly out of it; his heavy mind lurches this way and that. He gives the impression of a writer bewildered by transitions, handling the larger ones with chapter divisions and others not at all. Short passages lifted from his fiction may or may not be representative of the whole: his explanations do not always square with his characters' behavior, his narrative lumber was often badly proportioned, ill-cut, poorly grained, mismatched and scored.

So Dreiser built to no great symbolic moments; but he has memorable small ones. They occur, unpretentiously, quite on the way to something grander, as we think of them at the time, as in the opening paragraphs of the first famous novel:

> When Caroline Meeber boarded the afternoon train for Chicago, her total outfit consisted of a small trunk, a cheap

imitation alligator-skin satchel, a small lunch in a paper box, and a yellow leather snap purse, containing her ticket, a scrap of paper with her sister's address in Van Buren Street and four dollars in money. It was in August, 1889. She was eighteen years of age, bright, timid, and full of the illusions of ignorance and youth. Whatever touch of regret at parting characterised her thoughts, it was certainly not for advantages now being given up. A gush of tears at her mother's farewell kiss, a touch in her throat when the cars clacked by the flour mill where her father worked by the day, a pathetic sigh as the familiar green environs of the village passed in review, and the threads which bound her so lightly to girlhood and home were irretrievably broken.

To be sure there was always the next station, where one might descend and return. There was the great city, bound more closely by these very trains which came up daily. Columbia City was not so very far away, even once she was in Chicago. What, pray, is a few hours—a few hundred miles? She looked at the little slip bearing her sister's address and wondered. She gazed at the green landscape, now passing in swift review, until her swifter thoughts replaced its impression with vague conjectures of what Chicago might be.

Not all of Dreiser's world, by any means, is intimated in this passage from *Sister Carrie,* but a generous part of it is. There is the youth's journey from village—past nature—to the city, from known deprivations to hoped-for privileges, the vague and simple emotions turned inward, the rootlessness; there is the author's strangely mixed compassion and detachment about all this. There is his documentary interest in time of day, apparel and possessions, history and machinery. There is his absorption in movement: geographic, and of human individuals in transit toward living.

It is a skillful beginning to the novel, and an introduction to the rest of Dreiser's fiction as well. For we are brought close immediately to the protagonist whose feelings about life will dominate the foreground of the tale, and we are also made aware of the city which has generated or given direction to the strongest of those feelings and on whose terms they are fated to work themselves out. With variations, this is the pattern that emerges early in all of the novels. (A partial exception is *The Bulwark,* a stray pigeon on many counts.) The Columbus, Ohio, where Jennie Gerhardt seeks her first job corresponds to Carrie's Chicago; it has 50,000 people in 1880, the novelist carefully informs us, and is the state capital, with a sumptuous hotel and a resident United States senator that promote in Jennie those longings for comfort and security better satisfied in Cleveland and later Chicago. The Cowperwood trilogy opens with young Frank, at ten years already sensible, vigorous, courageous, defiant, and "forever pondering, pondering," looking straight toward the career in money that his native Philadelphia seems irresistibly to offer. In *The "Genius"* it is Eugene Witla and Chicago; in *An American Tragedy* the dreamy Clyde Griffiths and a very metropolitan Kansas City. Private longings and the public arena—Dreiser's scale is both intimate and vast. He was the first powerful American novelist of the emotions, inferior to Hawthorne and James in the capacity to analyze them but superior to both in re-creating their texture. And before him only *Moby-Dick* and James's international novels had been drawn on so prodigious a scale: for the voyages between oceans and continents, now a commerce with cities.

A part of Dreiser's achievement rests in his having joined the two spheres, in having shown how passion may be at once personal and social. The yearnings of his major characters *belong* palpably to the city. So tiny and shadowy is the settlement in *The Scarlet Letter* that one easily forgets whether it is meant to be Boston or Salem, but the same doubt is almost inconceivable in Dreiser's fiction. At the same time, very much as in the Hawthorne novel, the course of passion in Dreiser's world is severely conditioned by the type of community in which it transpires. The various adulteries, liaisons, flirtations, and clandestine desirings of his characters are born or nourished in the peculiarly sensuous atmosphere of the city, live feverishly in the anonymous cubicles the city provides and eventually die from either a natural boredom or the city-bred logistical difficulties of moving, quartering, and supplying all one's women. "The city has its cunning wiles," observes Dreiser of Carrie's pilgrimage to Chicago. The statement is redundant, amateurish, sententious—and completely true to his feelings. "There are large forces which allure with all the soulfulness of expression possible in the most cultured human. The gleam of a thousand lights is often as effective as the persuasive light in a wooing and fascinating eye. Half the undoing of the unsophisticated and natural mind is accomplished by forces wholly superhuman. A blare of sound, a roar of life, a vast array of human hives, appeal to the astonished senses in equivocal terms." He is describing the emotional spectacle that throughout the quarter-century of his best work held him entranced.

The sense of painful wonder that the bare physical immensity of a great city can arouse in the provincial soul Dreiser himself first experienced when he was twelve. The Chicago of 1884 excited and frightened him, and on a trip three years later he began to identify his ambitions with that expanding metropolis. New York too, as late as his early twenties, struck him as "huge and powerful and terrible," as he afterward remembered it, and the two characters that most nearly re-enact those journeys, Carrie Meeber and Eugene Witla, marvel as he must have marveled at the prairie gauntness of Chicago and the island splendor of Manhattan. One is always lured in this way to seek the underlying parallel in Dreiser's life, so autobiographical was he and so affectingly tormented was that life. In his

work this temptation is inescapable, I think; and our in-
clination to read his tales as chronicles of an American era
or as illustrations of Nietzschean and social-Darwinist axioms
is more likely to grow than disappear. Such extrapolations
are not necessarily unfortunate, and Dreiser himself would
surely have welcomed them. But it is well to be certain
when we are talking about his novels as artifacts and when
we are not, and though many blunders have taught us this
caution with Melville and Whitman, we have not quite
learned it with Dreiser. Relying on that writer's autobiographical accounts, for instance, Matthiessen has said
that Chicago "was to be etched in [Dreiser's] brain in an
endless series of pictures of tall new towers silhouetted
against the lake, of the black oily river as he hung along
its bridges, of the immeasurable energy that pulsated from
the grain elevators and railroad yards and the vast central
building of the Board of Trade." These etchings do appear in
his nonfictional writings, and here and there in his novels,
particularly in The "Genius," where rather self-consciously
he 'paints' (or etches) an urban landscape. However, the
visual memories of Chicago and other American cities which
Dreiser leans on most heavily for novelistic purposes are
of ground floors rather than skylines, seldom of tall towers
or grain elevators but commonly of low-lying residences.

There *is* architecture in Dreiser's novels, but it is domestic
not public, and less important visually than thematically.
This admirer of Alfred Stieglitz had a sharp eye for the
urban pictorial, but the eye was not really "marvellous," as
Dorothy Dudley claimed. He saw quickly, wrote rapidly,
was not in the least concerned to reproduce meticulously in
words the rich paintings set before us in James's late novels.
His art may be that of a Hopper, as Alfred Kazin suggests,
or a Sloan, whose grosser techniques and more darkly romantic realism seem to me more comparable to Dreiser's own;
it is in any case an art of the bold sketch, with the artist
going swiftly to what he wants. The architecture Dreiser

chooses to present in this way is interestingly similar from novel to novel.

It is an architecture of façades, entrances, and interiors. The fact is, of course, telling. To have *access*—to the beckoning rooms of love and power—is overwhelmingly the passion gripping Dreiser's characters. They are outside, craving, and they want to be inside, enjoying. Theirs are the yearnings of children, prolonged into adulthood by a civilization that insists on the infantile joys of possession but allows only a charmed few to possess. At first, still largely guileless, artless, drawn by simple feelings within and apparently natural attractions of beauty without, they move as if in a spell toward the mansions of privilege. Clyde Griffiths, for example,

> found himself ambling on and on until suddenly he was out of the business district again and in touch with a wide and tree-shaded thoroughfare of residences, the houses of which, each and every one, appeared to possess more room space, lawn space, general ease and repose and dignity even than any with which he had ever been in contact. In short, as he sensed it from this brief inspection of its very central portion, it seemed a very exceptional, if small city street—rich, luxurious even. So many imposing wrought-iron fences, flower-bordered walks, grouped trees and bushes, expensive and handsome automobiles either beneath porte-cochères within or speeding along the broad thoroughfare without.

This is the first of many walks Clyde takes from the obscure districts of Lycurgus, New York, to gaze at the bright exteriors of wealth. The scene has parallels in all but one of the other major novels. Jennie is "overawed" at the magnificent lobby of the Columbus hotel, Carrie is wholly enchanted by the lawns, entrance-ways, and glimpsed interiors of "palaces" along the North Shore Drive, Eugene by the "splendid houses" on Michigan and other avenues. Of the principal characters only Frank Cowperwood is not similarly awe-struck, but a cardinal point of his character is that he not be visibly overwhelmed by anything, and we learn all the same that he remembers his early visits to the homes of Butler the politician and others on fashionable Girard Avenue in Philadelphia and afterward builds his own house with an unusually "arresting" façade.

One of Dreiser's relentless ironies is that these souls are always permitted some access to the social world whose façades they have admired but never win the full approval which they hoped that entrance would effect. Always, in what they most desire, they fail. Dreiser piles up plausible reasons for their failure: weak will or untoward circumstances, Clyde's inadequacies and then Roberta's tumble from the rowboat. And yet the aristocrats' unwillingness to accept an agreeable young Jennie or Clyde remains imperfectly explained. At an advanced point in the protagonist's social progress, realistic explanations become curiously irrelevant: he is simply destined to lose, in a fate only more totally imposed than that facing James's heroes and heroines, only less insistently explicit than that facing Faulkner's. The fact that Dreiser did not know very intimately the lives of the pedigreed rich helps us to understand the mystery but does not help us decide whether the mystery serves a literary end. In fact it does. The inscrutability of the world of privilege is a main element in what becomes from book to book a parable of the city.

Once there was a young man (in some versions a young woman) who found his home restrictive and left at the first chance for the center of the city. A creature of nature and custom, there he hoped to discover freedom from irksome restraint and also the approval of society. (Some say falsely that he sought only self-indulgence.) The great Mansion lured him; it seemed to promise both liberty and acceptance. He longed to enter.

There came a woman from inside the great Mansion who

opened the door for him. But by this act she jeopardized her place in the Mansion. This was just, for the Mansion was Christian and like her new companion she was a Pagan. Wishing to be secure and yet to revolt, they turned elsewhere in the city to the Secret Room, where they could worship the gods of nature. But chance and the power of privilege betrayed them. The insider was compelled to choose between one god and many. She chose, unhappily. The outsider, given no choice, was driven from the Mansion.

The least allegorical of writers, nonetheless Dreiser returned to this story so often as to give it the force of allegory. For him it was the primordial tale of modern life, a tale which he could only repeat (with variations) since he could deduce no useful principles for conduct from it. The fundamental truth it appeared to demonstrate—who could be certain?—was that life in society was a trap. Of this truth the city was at once emblem and circumstance. "What a tangle life was," thinks Eugene, as in the pain of her child-bearing the sorrows of Angela's life and of his own merge in one great universal sorrow; and the sentiment echoes through all of the novels. Eugene's entanglements are many: his art, his business career, his relations with friends and women and himself have all become snarled. But one conflict has been common to them all—between conventionality and independence, the strangle hold of custom and the liberations of free action. This is the controlling theme of *The "Genius,"* whose thickly autobiographical stretches made for some of Dreiser's shrillest and also some of his most movingly impassioned writing, revealing how critical this theme was for him. Here the conflict is dramatized in parallel actions. Both the struggles between Eugene and his wife Angela and between Suzanne Dale and her mother are presented as inescapable clashes between fiercely independent and fiercely conventional personalities. Eugene is an artist, "pagan to the core"; Suzanne is possessed of "hard anarchic, unsocial thoughts." Angela and Mrs. Dale are managing types, who try implacably to discipline the two rebels as they have themselves been disciplined by their middle-class culture. Eventually Suzanne yields to her mother, in a denouement shaped more to Dreiser's past than to his characters', but the novelist's sympathies are overwhelmingly behind Eugene's struggle to be free.

The widowed Mrs. Dale, rich, of a famous New York family, owns many houses but prefers Daleview, the ancestral estate on Staten Island overlooking Manhattan and the harbor. Eugene is an occasional guest there until his passion erupts for Suzanne, whose mother then forbids him to enter the great house. The would-be lovers resolve to live privately in a studio, but the dream never materializes. Compelled to announce this plan, they are shocked to discover how vehemently Mrs. Dale and Angela react against it. The compromise with conventionality they looked to quickly vanishes; to enter society is to surrender one's freedom.

Because Eugene is "a painter," the secret room he conspires to share with Suzanne is to be "a studio"; but the word is also their attempt to romanticize a meeting-place for illicit love. The secret room in the other novels has less glamor, is usually a flat in an apartment-house or an apartment in a private dwelling. But whether as the comfortable place Drouet finds for Carrie on the West Side of Chicago, the ampler suite on the North Side where Les Kane installs Jennie, or the old-fashioned bedroom Roberta rents at Clyde's insistence in Lycurgus, the room always lays claim to reputability. Of none is this truer than the Philadelphia chamber to which Frank Cowperwood is reduced to taking Aileen Butler, in a house of assignation. There the red-brick façade trimmed in white stone and the furnishings of the lovers' room ("showy but cleanly," parading the "commonplace idea of luxury which then prevailed") protest the respectability of the establishment, even as the Pinkertons (in the name of an implacable law) force the proprietress to reveal the whereabouts of the lovers. Even in their utmost conspiracy against the Mansion, the rebels still submit to the values it inspires.

Inside the room, moreover, the lovers are themselves divided in spirit. In that "Paradise" they love wildly, and they worry. For various reasons and in varying degrees they are shackled to the world of conventional opinion, at the same time that they pursue or drift into passion. Rejoicing in every "concealing, rewarding feverish night" with Roberta, while their clandestine affair is still young, Clyde thinks continually of his truly privileged relatives, the Griffiths, "and all they represented in his life and that of the city. Their great house closed and silent, except for gardeners and an occasional chauffeur or servant visible as he walked from time to time past the place, was the same as a shrine to him, nearly —the symbol of that height to which by some turn of fate he might still hope to attain." One day after her affair begins with Drouet, Carrie looks in the mirror (a sign, as in Hawthorne, that we are about to witness the truth). There "she saw a prettier Carrie than she had seen before; she looked into her mind, a mirror prepared of her own and the world's opinions, and saw a worse." The statement which follows defines Carrie's predicament and that of the other lovers: "Between these two images she wavered, hesitating which to believe."

The word "believe" seems to sound the one uncharacteristic note. For Dreiser's heroines and heroes are not really concerned with belief; but they think they are. They think that if only they can perceive the truth, can make the right decision, they will escape their predicaments. They are astonishing rationalists, true Americans, true Europeans. Whereas the objective fact about them is, Dreiser insists, that they "drift" or plunge as the great universal forces shove them from within or without. Their entrapment within the city is a spectacle for philosophic deliberation—but also for rejoicing. In Dreiser these moods are not easily separable: his fiction, even the meanest of it, is so impressive because he could link the particular swelling of emotion to general causes. But his fiction stirs us, as that of few other American writers can do, mainly because he celebrates natural human feeling. He has never been convinced of its inherent rightness, he simply *assumes* it. Dreiser is, in this respect, genuinely an innocent, as all of his heroes and heroines are innocents. He is aware of disastrous results, but not of evil. He is utterly secular, utterly profane, withal a transcendentalist.

Carrie's secret room in Chicago overlooks a park, Jennie's is near the lake. The touches are incidental, but not wholly so. Living close to nature is what the secret room offers, a nature interior but with its outward correspondences. Long passages near the beginning of her novel tell of Jennie Gerhardt's affinities with the natural world. "Where the sunlight was warm and the shadows flecked with its splendid radiance she delighted to wonder at the pattern of it, to walk where it was most golden, and follow with instinctive appreciation the holy corridors of the trees." Of all Dreiser's women she is the most saintlike, is in fact entirely a saint. Seeing her family in want, she accepts with few misgivings a surreptitious life with Lester that will eliminate that want. Some of the other lovers are a good deal more conscience-ridden, for example Roberta Alden, but they are all presented as innately good individuals. Even Frank Cowperwood's drive for power and Eugene Witla's for success are essentially ingenuous. They are creatures of Emerson's imagination, and of Whitman's.

But though they are not corrupted by society, as Emerson's were, they are painfully coerced by it. In Dreiser there is none of Emerson's sense that the individual can rise superior to society, not even in the manipulative career of Cowperwood, who is repeatedly struck down, thwarted, and only fleetingly through his money ventures manages to establish any clear relationship to a world outside himself; nor is there any sense as in Whitman that the individual can fuse his experience with that of any human group. Dreiser's individual is always at bottom adrift in the metropolis. He can only salvage some part of what he is born with, his emotive nature, and hope to give it spasmodic expression. His desire is not to be self-reliant but to be free; not to fulfill himself through adventure, in the manner of the Romantic hero, but to preserve some passional identity. So it is that sexual relations become diluted in Dreiser's fiction from pure ends into means as well, largely meaningless for the women and sometimes compulsive for the men. The love that begins in feeling ends in fear—of the "world's opinion." And that opinion, in the guise of conscience, easily invades the secret room. Conscience, in Dreiser's view, is absolutely social: Carrie's is constructed of "past environment, habit, convention." The Pinkertons need not tap at the door; the Mansion need only exist, and exert its overwhelming appeal.

In Dreiser's cities that is the function of the Mansion: to stand resplendently, to epitomize success, which is to say the approval of the existing social order. Whatever increase in freedom it seems to promise is largely illusory, as Clyde Griffiths discovers inside the Finchleys' home. The servility the Finchley world demands and its fundamental coldness are wonderfully evoked by the scene in the big kitchen one night when Clyde, seated at a servants' table by Sondra, stares wild-eyed at the rich display of pots and pans and silver service. His dalliance there with the daughter of the mansion is entirely chaste, "without lust, just the desire to constrain and fondle a perfect object." Meanwhile, the pagan Roberta lies in her room across the city; yet life with her offers no clear-cut alternative. Indeed the very character of the secret room foretells the outcome: *it too belongs to the city.* The pagans cannot make love under the elms or on the beach; to live according to nature they must occupy a room. And having surrendered so much of nature to custom, they find they must give up still more. Passion leads to Roberta's pregnancy, to Eugene's exhaustion, and in the web of social convention in the city these also become snares.

But one cannot live outside the city. Dreiser sees small-town or rural life for the most part as "narrow," and pushes it away toward the edge of his fiction. That average human beings should be lured to the city and trapped there—that is the dilemma. And while aspects of their travail draw from Dreiser a certain pleasure and thoughtfulness, the spectacle as a whole arouses chiefly his involved, compassionate regret. Dreiser bears comparison with Conrad and Hardy at many points, but above all in this; and in this he contrasts sharply with Lawrence, whose obsessive fear that passion would be killed in the modern world resembles Dreiser's in some respects but whose aloofness from his characters differs conspicuously from Dreiser's helpless identification with them. For all Dreiser's naïveté and because of it, he manages to convey the incredible poignance of lives in which feelings always overflow the vessels built to contain them, in which the deeper passions are always being channeled and dammed up. "O burning human appetite and desire on every hand!" In the city desire is increased, made furtive, and finally destroyed. And there is no way out.

V

Grassblades Assassinated

E. E. CUMMINGS

While Eliot and William Carlos Williams had preceded him there, no one is so likely to seem the first contemporary American city poet as Cummings. Like any impression, this one obscures part of the truth; but like any impression either vivid or general, it is essentially true. Unlike the author of "Prufrock," Cummings usually addresses himself to an identifiable (and as it happens, an American) city. And unlike Williams, whose first lines on Manhattan antedate his by three or four years, Cummings appears never to have regarded that city from any distance, certainly not from across the river. Whitman might be said to have prophesied his coming: *Others will enter . . . will watch . . . will see . . . Fifty years hence.* But Cummings, Whitman's poetic heir in numerous other respects, strikes us as never having crossed by the ferry. He was, somehow, always there, between the lower East and West walls of the citadel. We greet word of his boyhood in suburban Cambridge ("Only a butterfly's glide" from the "semiwilderness")—or of his doing summer chores year after year on a sprawling New Hampshire farm—with disbelief. Nothing could seem more anomalous.

That suburb and farm were really not so anomalous may be gathered from the profusion of his verses to Nature. Still it is easier for us to think of Cummings' hymns to Spring as the result of excursions from a city flat than as impulsive outpourings under the White Mountain evergreens. Our impression rests, of course, on tone—something in the artifice with which he speaks of trees, rather more in the assortment of voices he brings to any subject. (Emerson, rather than Whitman, furnished the prophecy: "Cities force growth and make men talkative and entertaining, but they make them artificial.") Of Cummings' many voices, two in particular sound notes of the city: irreverence and display, the urge to affront and the urge to dazzle.

The group he wished to affront had not existed as a solid, stable body in Whitman's time: the urban, literate, largely (and vaguely) Protestant-Christian, prosperous, nationalistic, complacent, and proper upper middle-class. Scandalizing the bourgeoisie was an old enough game in Europe, but to play it there had to be money-makers who could read, or whose wives, children, or neighbors could, and none of these were to be found in any numbers in America until the 1860s. By the 1870s Howells could depend on a readership of the wives; by the 1920s, Cummings on that of the rebellious children. Especially in his satiric poems Cummings took into his confidence those who, like himself, were young, iconoclastic, bookish, excited by art, and both amused and exasperated by the burghers' culture from which most of them sprang. These children, not their parents, were his real audience, the one he tried to entertain and the only one educated enough to get the jokes. Soon after the war, before or after brief travels to Europe, small numbers of them settled in Greenwich Village, joined by larger numbers in spirit. The Bohemia that coalesced south of James's old Washington Square became a base of postwar operations against the absurdities of American conventionalism, the Bohemian spirit the instrument Cummings employed for his one-man assault. The fact that he lived in and near the Village (how the urban ironies multiply in *that* name!) for some forty years, save only for oc-

casional trips abroad, merely confirms what his poetry leads
us to expect.

One side of this spirit was mockingly negative. (The
question whether Cummings is thus hoist on his own *un-*
prefix has a mild relevance.) It was anti-respectability, anti-
solemnity, anti-marriage, anti-patriotism, anti-commercialism,
anti-fraudulence, anti-prudery, anti-bourgeois decorum. Many
of the poems in this vein have been among his most popular,
a phenomenon suggesting how nicely he had gauged or represented his audience. They often take the form of salutations,
as with beer stein aloft. *Here's to*—the American merger of
the patriotic and commercial:

> my country, 'tis of
>
> you, land of the Cluett
> Shirt Boston Garter and Spearmint
> Girl With The Wrigley Eyes(of you
> land of the Arrow Ide
> and Earl &
> Wilson
> Collars) of you i
> sing:land of Abraham Lincoln and Lydia E. Pinkham,
> land above all of Just Add Hot Water And Serve—
> from every B. V. D.
>
> let freedom ring
>
> amen. . . .

And here's to battle enthusiasms back at the snug old home-
stead:

> . . . my
> mother hoped that
>
> i would die etcetera
> bravely of course my father used

> to become hoarse talking about how it was
> a privilege and if only he
> could . . .

And here's to truckling opportunism:

> Humanity i love you
> because you would rather black the boots of
> success than enquire whose soul dangles from his
> watch-chain which would be embarrassing for both
>
> parties . . .

These salutes are fired off, these toasts proposed, as it were, from one of the *bistros* below 14th Street. The shots are all tracers, with the double purpose of damaging the enemy and showing where they came from. The *I*—although (and *because*) it is lower-case—in each of these poems is prominent. That de-emphasis affirms the poet's own freedom from conventionality, of course, but it also offers another means of offending puritan sensibilities.

For very young Bohemians, a poolroom will serve. The voice of one early poem tells us,

> when i am in Boston, i do not speak.
> and i sit in the click of ivory balls. . . .

Meanwhile, out in his suburb, sit those estimable women who since their appearance in his first collection of poems have become familiar symbols of banal, uncreative, conventional bourgeois female minds:

> the Cambridge ladies who live in furnished souls
> are unbeautiful and have comfortable minds
> (also, with the church's protestant blessings
> daughters, unscented shapeless spirited)

These are the opening lines of a (slightly untraditional) sonnet, slyly followed in the collection by sonnets on harlots. Cummings' women of the lupanar (the archaism is Drei-

ser's) are "Unspontaneous" too and so contrast with the
freely passionate lovers he celebrates in lyric after lyric; but
his portraits of prostitutes could also be guaranteed (as when
he labels one gallery "Five Americans") to pain the solid
citizenry.

Over against all the ridiculous bourgeois sobrieties Cummings set his own enthusiasms. Most particularly in work
from the early 1920s on into the '30s he gave literary expression not to the dreary or pathetic or morally questionable
aspects of the Bohemian temper, but to its vitality. The dis-
reputable language of the street is alive:

> oil tel duh woil doi sez

> . . . but what i mean is Nobody Understands Her RERLY

> take it from me kiddo

To be "beautiful or/deep or generous" is to be alive ("whistle
that/sing that yell that spell/that out big . . ."). Even city-
bred voyeurisms can be alive, if the women are—whether on
the streets:

> hanged

> if n
> y in a real hot spell
> with o

> man

> what bubbies going
> places on such
> babies aint plenty
> good enough for

i

eu
can have
you

rope

or in the burlesque house, where Sally Rand danced

handsomely who did because she could what the movies try
to do because they can't i mean move

Sensuously graceful movement, evidence of vitality, may
also be had in the appearance of a poem on the printed page.
This is one function of Cummings' radically manipulated
typography. But from his earliest verse experiments Cummings had grasped still another end which a greater freedom
with language might promote. He could not only produce
new effects with old experiences, as in the "hanged" poem
above, but also restructure those experiences. Of all his
pyrotechnics, this is one of the most original and interesting,
short-lived though it was in its initial, "purer" forms. His
attempt was to expropriate for poetry certain of the ideas
underlying modern abstract painting and sculpture. This
venture was quite separate from his attack on smug Americans, except in being—like Bohemianism—a form of rebellion against the traditional. Like Bohemianism also, it
found its most congenial and in some respects indispensable
home in the objects, energies, and displacements of the city.

The nature of this innovation may be seen in two short
early poems. In the following lines the poet perceives external
reality, conventionally, as though it were human:

                    . . . the city
          wakes
          with a song upon her
          mouth having death in her eyes

In another poem from the same group of "Impressions," however, the city reality is perceived as dynamic structure:

> writhe and
> gape of tortured
>
> perspective
> rasp and graze of splintered
>
> normality
>   crackle and
>   sag
> of planes   clamors of
> collision
> collapse . . .

Except later, in a closing stanza, the city is not personified; it is geometrized. Here the vocabulary of painting (*perspective, planes, dimension*) indicates the consciousness and specificity of his intent—in contrast, for instance, to the more inherently graphic imaginations of Stephen Crane and Kafka, as I have suggested, or to those of James and Faulkner. The effort is really too conscious, most of us would say, too contrived to allow us much besides an analytical satisfaction, too dependent on the isolated instance. But it opens up possibilities, as Cummings' little experiments so often did, some of which he went on to explore.

Although the poet's own paintings are not well known, his fondness for painting is. Almost from the moment Continental modernism gained notoriety in the United States with the Armory exhibition of 1913, Cummings had shown himself fascinated with it, and with its implications for poetry. (Thus launched in New York and carried forward there by artists, dealers, purchasers, museum directors, and critics, 'modern art' has ever since connoted to Americans a distinctly urban product.) In a recent study, Barry Marks has rightly emphasized Cummings' absorption during those years in the new art. While other American poets of the period were renewing verse by means of the more traditional resources of imagery and the spoken language, Marks points out, Cummings was borrowing what he could from the abstract painters and sculptors. His Harvard commencement address of 1915, essaying parallels among the various major arts, dealt with Cubism and Futurism, with Matisse, Cézanne, Duchamp, Brancusi, and the Armory Show. These interests affected his literary judgments and his poetry, notably in his treatment of a poem as a visual structure whose parts are properly subject to fragmenting and recombining for added meaning and effect.

To these observations may be added another: that the influence appears too in Cummings' interest in types of perception most nearly identifiable with types in the non-literary arts. Thus in the poem above beginning "writhe and/gape," the Futurist qualities are evident mainly in the representation of a city whose normal condition is seen as "splintered" and which is then reconstructed as sagging planes. The whole process (reinforced by appropriate noise) makes concrete the artist's sense of movement and energy in the metropolis. (The slightly eccentric spacing of the words adds to the sense of motion, though in this instance the visual is secondary to the perceptual.) Similarly, in another poem from *Tulips and Chimneys* (1923), a stanza presents experience distorted in an expressionist manner akin to that in Stephen Crane:

> any skyscraper
> bulges in the looseness of morning
> but in twilight becomes
> unutterably crisp

Again, in the interestingly eclectic Number XI from the collection *& [AND]* (1925), in a group entitled "Post Impressions," the poet minimizes the traditional identity of the object (through the interpenetration of the speaker's senses, and the flow of experience through and around him); he tries also to destroy traditional notions of form (here, chiefly the barrier between prose and verse) and to give color the prominence it can have in painting, as in the decorative brilliance of a Matisse; and he employs elements of exaggerative fantasy (*my eyes go into . . . the dark long cool tunnel*) as André Breton and other Surrealists were just then beginning to use them. Here is the first of four main sections:

> my eyes are fond of the east side
> as i lie asleep my eyes go into Allen street the dark
> long cool tunnel of raving colour, on either side the
> windows are packed with hardslippery greens and
> helplessbaby blues and stic-ky chromes and pretty-
> lemons and virginal pinks and wealthy vermilion
> and breathless-scarlet,dark colours like 'cellos keen
> fiddling colours colours cOOler than harps colours
> p r i c k i n glike piccolos thumPing colours like a
> bangofpiano colours which,are,the,flowery pluckings
> of a harpsichord colours of Pure percussion colours-
> like-trumpets they(writhe they,struggleinweird chords
> of humorous,fury heapingandsqueezing tum-bling-
> scratchingcrowd ingworming each by screetching
> Each)on either side the street's DarkcOOllonGBody
> windows, are. clenched. fists of tint.

Other sections send out into the East Side the speaker's mouth, ears, and genitals.

The result is a prosepoem both dazzling and bawdy, a double breach in decorum, a double assertion of the poet's daring—and of the splendor the city offers in forms both natural and unnatural. These oppositions insist on each other in Cummings' universe, they fasten and feed on one another. This is the key to much of his work and its great single irony. He must scorn the burgesses because they disavow the free life he values; but that life takes an inordinate part of its value from having been disavowed. Bohemia without Uptown is inconceivable. So it is that he forever gibes at the stuffed shirts, or proclaims not just that erotic love is lovely but that it is absolutely, luxuriously so; he must announce within the first five minutes to his Harvard listeners, in 1915 or 1952, that he is indecently addicted to the new art or the old burlesque. Comic he is, and capable of swift modulations in tone; but so often one hears in his poetry a cry of stiff extremes, either truculence or ecstasy. Like many romantics, including Whitman, Cummings was possessed of a strong hygienic impulse: he wanted the world *clean.* Things made must be segregated from things born, syntax from feeling, the astronomer's lecture (another fealty to Whitman) from the immeasurable night. He is pinned, however, against the terms of his own equation. Sally Rand's naturalness is also artifice, protest is couched in language, love affirmed in the sonnet, Brancusi on the page reduced and tamed. While Spring comes and lovers entwine, a rancid hurdy-gurdy gurgles and thumps. Nature exists in his poems, for the most part, *because* the city exists; one is significant insofar as the other is.

The significance of Cummings' city and nature rarely soars, because from the first he has seldom passed beyond their surfaces. His bourgeoisie remain rudimentary symbols, as do the rebellions down at McSorley's Bar or the Old Howard; and his extrapolations from painting and sculpture remain mostly ends in themselves. As a vessel of serious comment, therefore, Cummings' city stands astonishingly close to the picturesque city of Howells. Yet Cummings' will endure while the other one crumbles to ruins for the literary archaeologist; indeed, the difference appears already. If we are to have surfaces, then let them *shine!* In this measure too, Cummings showed himself to have the greater wit.

VI

Lost City

F. SCOTT FITZGERALD

" 'You talk glibly,' " says a minor character to the hero of
This Side of Paradise, to which the hero responds passion-
ately, " 'It's not all rubbish.' " An obstacle to appreciating
F. Scott Fitzgerald—perhaps *the* obstacle—is glib talk, that
verbal ease of his which forever brings into question the
depth of the imagination behind.

Our revived interest in Fitzgerald's fiction since the Second World War has a decided social basis, to be sure, in the
hedonistic lives we seem to have copied from old photographs
of that first great postwar dissipation. And there has been the
normal upswing in a writer's reputation after his death.
That upswing has lasted somewhat longer than usual, perhaps because his death was of a kind perennially appealing
to American intellectuals: the artist damned by dollars. Fitzgerald's brand of victimization, however, was not Melville's.
It was a fate certainly known nowhere in the world in any
age on the kind of scale familiar to the contemporary American artist—damned not by too few but by too many dollars,
damned by an audience not too small but too massive, too
appreciative and too curious. The phenomenal public ac-
claim of Fitzgerald's first novel in 1920 may be said, indeed,
to have signaled the change in the American writer's for-

tunes. In *America's Coming of Age* of 1915, and again in his Mark Twain biography five years later, Van Wyck Brooks could speak of the artist's doom among Philistines in a social indictment that required only his eloquence to be accepted. And yet almost at the moment *The Ordeal of Mark Twain* came from the press, the reality behind that allegation was altering. An audience only slightly less Philistine than in the days of Melville or Twain began to crave good prose. It did not want art so much as the titillations of art, as some four decades of the mass media have now proven, but with increasing literacy its standards were rising, and it began to have the money to pay for finished products.

Fitzgerald's attractiveness, though, cannot be explained wholly on these social grounds, or on those of his flights with Zelda or the subsequent wreckage of both their lives. For our generation as for his, he has charmed mainly through his art. Whether his charm will falter once the supporting social conditions drop away, as it faltered for a time in the thirties, will naturally depend on the quality of that art, its final seriousness, its discernments. In all that remains to be said by way of critical judgment on Fitzgerald's work, nothing seems more to the point than an inquiry into the significance of his "lost city."

Almost exactly the same age as Cummings, acquiring a public in the same postwar years, Fitzgerald gave from the first a similar impression of himself as having broken with his literary predecessors. Truer than not, the impression comes importantly, as it did for Cummings, from the ease with which he moves among things of the city, from his lack of emotional attachments to worlds beyond or apart from or alien to it, as Melville had the sea, Faulkner (even then) the American South, James the consciousness. He would appear to resemble Dreiser in his indifference (again, like Cummings') to the rural America that slopes off from the edge of the great cities; but he has little of Dreiser's awe at their novelty, and because he does not consider the passage into the city peculiarly wonderful, he shows none of Dreiser's despair at finding the place an ash-heap. New York *was* new —and wonderful—to Fitzgerald at one time, but cities were not. He had been a child in St. Paul and Buffalo, had breathed the thickly urbane atmosphere of an Eastern preparatory school and then of Princeton, with its dual orientation toward Southern wealth and downtown Manhattan pleasures. The spirit of this upbringing along with most of its circumstantial details went straight into his fiction.

While his novels have their share of provincials come to the metropolis, since Howells' day the species has varied. Most of them have journeyed to the city not from the country but from smaller cities. In the earlier novels they are drawn to New York—Amory Blaine from Minneapolis and the rich Chicago colony at Lake Geneva, Wisconsin (though his birthplace is unspecified); Gloria Gilbert Patch from Kansas City (Anthony Patch already a Manhattanite or from one of the affluent Connecticut tributaries); and Tom Buchanan from Chicago, Daisy and Jordan Baker both from Louisville, and Nick Carraway from a far-Midwestern city northwest of Chicago. *Tender Is the Night* takes Nicole Warren from Chicago to Zurich—described as "not unlike an American city"—and her husband Dick Diver there from Buffalo. In the completed portions of *The Last Tycoon*, interestingly, although there are vague allusions to lives formerly led elsewhere, the only definite information we have is of beginnings and ends in Hollywood.

The connotations of place do function in his novels, but for the most part Fitzgerald refuses to identify his characters closely with their geographical origins. One reason is almost certainly to increase the air of romantic mystery about them, as with Gatsby, who has risen to his courtly eminence from an unnamed locality in North Dakota, a prosaic fact that Nick and the reader do not learn until late in the novel and that Gatsby's neighbors never do. While the theme of the

American Midwest against the East is integral to *The Great
Gatsby,* however, and receives flickering attention in all save
the last of the other novels, it is conceived in just those broad
geographical terms rather than being fastened to city and
hinterlands.

Fitzgerald's characters are often associated with place but
are nearly as often separated from it. (One remembers, inescapably, the Fitzgeralds' staccato diary of notations on their
restless migrations year after year from hotel to hotel to
hotel.) The characters may impress us as cosmopolitan, but
a Prince Amerigo or a Mme. de Vionnet reminds us how
wanting they are in significant urban attachments for that.
Typical are the peregrinations of Beatrice Blaine through
America and Europe, on which the novelist comments, "The
Blaines were attached to no city." Neither are they attached
to other kinds of place:

> Eight hours from Princeton Amory sat down by the Jersey
> roadside and looked at the frost-bitten country. Nature
> as a rather coarse phenomenon composed largely of flowers
> that, when closely inspected, appeared moth-eaten, and
> of ants that endlessly traversed blades of grass, was al-
> ways disillusioning; nature represented by skies and waters
> and far horizons was more likeable.

Nature far off is all right, but not close up. And it is less
compelling by a good deal than the games of boys and young
men: autumn makes Amory think of a prep-school "battle,"
and of another one in France. His indifference to nature,
foreshadowing that of Fitzgerald's other protagonists, is almost total.

With no real links to birthplaces or cities, then, and none
to nature, to what if anything are these characters attached?
To their bathrooms, one is tempted to reply. Only one hero
actually has this attachment, but in various respects he stands
as representative. This lord of the bath is Anthony Patch, the

interior of whose Manhattan apartment is described at what looks like disproportionate length in *The Beautiful and Damned*. Of his huge bachelor's quarters on 52nd Street near 5th Avenue the bedroom and bathroom are "the heart and core." Both rooms are "immense." The bedroom has a great canopied bed and a thick soft carpet of crimson velvet that Anthony enjoys walking on in his bare feet. The splendid bathroom, however, means much more to him. It is "gay, bright, extremely habitable." Framed photographs of four beautiful actresses decorate the walls, together with a print showing an expanse of snow and a "cold and formidable sun." There is a low, large bathtub equipped with a bookholder, a wall wardrobe bulging with neckties and linen, a luxurious rug like the one in his bedroom, and a three-sided mirror. Over a page and a half are given to one instance of his leisurely bathing and dressing there. "It was his pride, this bathroom."

The sitting room of the apartment—with its fireplace, deep-stuffed chair and lounge—is less important to Anthony, almost an appendage of the inner rooms beyond. With its wall of a thousand books, it could serve as a study, were Anthony so minded. But though he loves his apartment, though he thinks with relief after entering it from the difficult streets of the city, *Here, after all, life began*, what he means by "life" has nothing about it so strenuous as the work which having a study implies. "Here," in his apartment, "he slept, breakfasted, read, and entertained." On an income of seven thousand a year, waiting for his grandfather's millions to drop, with occasional trips to the Ritz-Carlton rooftop restaurant or to his broker's, Anthony passes his days of refined self-indulgence. Narcissistic as his existence appears, it looks out to the world in a peculiar way. Much as when he apes before his bathroom mirror the posture of an athlete in an advertisement, his life as a whole is a succession of poses for others to admire, or at least to take for the real man. To his grandfather he pretends to be en-

gaged in "historical research," to his friends he pretends to
hold serious opinions on literature and living, to Gloria before marriage he pictures himself as committed to the career
of a gentleman aristocrat and after marriage to a personal
courage she soon learns he does not possess. "Life began"
for Anthony in his apartment because it is there, sitting near
his books, attended in bed by his manservant, bathing sensuously, that his fictions about himself come nearest to corre-
sponding with reality. That is what he is most deeply attached
to, insofar as his attachment has any depth: images of himself.

In this respect he typifies Fitzgerald's major characters.
They are all on view, they all wish a certain likeness of themselves to be seen, all of them stand eternally before their
triptych mirrors. Or before the movie cameras, one might
better say—for their state of mind is one we ascribe with
rough justice to Hollywood. That Fitzgerald was writing
movie scripts out there while cracking up has impressed
commentators with its social and biographical aptness; Hollywood is, after all, the city where the national talent goes
to pot, etc. But the fascination of fatal possibilities in his
entente with the studios easily obscures for us the question
of specific Hollywood influences on his fiction. For an ap-
praisal of his art this is the more relevant question, and one
that yields instructive answers. Long before *The Last Tycoon,*
before Hollywood had a voice or was even a city, it had in
fact exerted its pull, had charmed this writer so uncommonly
susceptible to charm. The results are not quite so predictable
as one may suppose.

The circumstantial evidence is hardly conclusive, but it
points the direction. In 1922 the twenty-five-year-old author
was discussing with movie agents a film of *This Side of
Paradise* (with himself and Zelda in the principal roles).
The following spring, he sold the movie rights to that novel.
Later *Gatsby* was purchased, and still later *Tender is the
Night* and the story "Babylon Revisited." His interest in

the process of film-making grew quickly, according to one biographer, after he watched the shooting of *Ben Hur* at Rome in the winter of 1924–25. Then early in 1927 he made the first voyage to the great Western capital, working there about three months on a script for a popular actress of the silent films. A subsequent trip, for Metro-Goldwyn-Mayer in 1931, left him "disillusioned and disgusted, vowing never to go back," but six years afterward he did go back, for what proved to be his last years, working hard on various script assignments to clear up his debts, with only intermittent trips back East.

It is easy to see both too much and too little in this attraction of nearly two decades to the American Babylon. Understandably, an overemphasis has come on the personal side, with Fitzgerald's final journey to the Los Angeles annex seeming variously a capitulation, a pilgrimage, in any case an inevitable and symbolic anti-climax to a life of heady drinking and spending. But it is also an error to minimize that attraction, to think of Fitzgerald's life in the East and the West as somehow disconnected, as though he had a New York (or Princeton) mentality for his real work and a quite separate, Hollywood mentality, functioning on a different level and by the well-paid hour, for the scripts. Certain facts do favor such a separation. Ostensibly the only literary results of his 1927 trip, for instance, were the story "Magnetism," published the next year, and the character in *Tender is the Night* eventually named Rosemary Hoyt, modeled on a young actress the author had met and admired in Los Angeles. Out of the second visit came only "Crazy Sunday," written upon his return East in 1932, and some notes for the novel that was to be the obvious and principal harvest of his concluding stay. Nevertheless, a careful look at the two novels composed after he had learned how to write for the camera shows that his practical experience in Hollywood had given him a new range of subject matter and had also altered his craft. That city was performing its wonders, and in ways only slightly mysterious.

Tender is the Night, overhauled and brought to completion following his 1931 assignment, reveals an imagination best described as cinematographic. This is, like any description of that novel, true unevenly. Malcolm Cowley's notes on the successive versions demonstrate with what pains and in what halting stages the book was constructed, and there seem to me plain internal signs that in his compositional labors during those tortured days Fitzgerald had grown more dependent than formerly on the stimulus of others' work. Despite his later disclaimer of stylistic debts to Hemingway, for instance, Chapter 3 in Book II of the final version, where Rosemary talks with Mrs. McKisco on the beach not far from Cannes, sways markedly to his friend's prose rhythms. (" 'He's nervous.' 'I'm not nervous,' disagreed McKisco. 'It just happens I'm not nervous at all.' ") The movie influence took various forms, from the inclusion of a Hollywood actress as a major character to the use of film sets as physical settings, from scenes in which movies are run off in private showings to other scenes in which a house interior impresses one of the characters as resembling nothing so much as a film set and as giving to parties there the "false-and-exalted" tone of its doubly artificial décor. Some of the minor characters seem so patently drawn from the special movieland repertoire of pasteboard types as to transpose effortlessly onto the screen, perhaps the best example being the psychiatrist Franz Gregorovius, who was indeed thus transposed in the American movie of a quarter-century afterward.

In *Tender is the Night* the cinema also affected the mode of perception. There are incidental, fragmentary moments: "For him time stood still and then every few years accelerated in a rush, like the quick rewind of a film. . . ." And there are larger moments, when motion-camera technology provides the medium through which an entire action is perceived. For example, the scene in which Rosemary asks Dick Diver to make love to her closes with this paragraph:

> "Good night, child. This is a damn shame. Let's drop it out of the picture." He gave her two lines of hospital patter to go to sleep on. "So many people are going to love you and it might be nice to meet your first love all intact, emotionally too. That's an old-fashioned idea, isn't it?" She looked up at him as he took a step toward the door; she looked at him without the slightest idea as to what was in his head, she saw him take another step in slow motion, turn and look at her again, and she wanted for a moment to hold him and devour him, wanted his mouth, his ears, his coat collar, wanted to surround him and engulf him; she saw his hand fall on the doorknob. Then she gave up and sank back on the bed. When the door closed she got up and went to the mirror, where she began brushing her hair, sniffling a little. One hundred and fifty strokes Rosemary gave it, as usual, then a hundred and fifty more. She brushed it until her arm ached, then she changed arms and went on brushing.

The triviality of Dick Diver's responses may distract us from Fitzgerald's genuine accomplishment in the passage—the secure handling of a distinctly visual point of view. The passage fails, destroying the scene, chiefly because the dialogue presents only banal emotions. It is written not just with the camera in mind but the great American softminded audience —written toward the movie pattern he knew, in short, rather than toward the novel at hand.

What could happen when he bent the new technology to his own fictive ends is evident here and there in that superb half-novel *The Last Tycoon*. When Monroe Stahr, sitting alone in his home late at night, finally reads the letter in which Kathleen says goodbye, at first he cannot believe she will stick to that and then decides she could—"and the whole adventure began to peel away even as he recapitulated it searchingly to himself. The car, the hill, the hat, the music, the letter itself, blew off like the scraps of tar paper from the rubble of his house. And Kathleen departed, packing up her remembered gestures, her softly moving head, her sturdy eager body, her bare feet in the wet swirling sand. The skies paled and faded—the wind and rain turned dreary, washing the silver fish back to sea. It was only one more day, and nothing was left except the pile of scripts upon the table." The visual perspective here is again that of photographed motion, but the cinematography is now integral to the writer's immediate aim, which is to suggest vividly and complexly the character's state of mind. The filmed images are not delivered as ends in themselves, as they are in the bedroom scene from *Tender is the Night;* they are absorbed, melted down into the flow of the art. The result is a passage at once subtle and moving.

Besides affording a subject matter, a new conception of scene, an added depth to his language, Hollywood quite probably helped keep Fitzgerald pointed toward certain kinds of notation he did best on the kinds of human beings he knew best. He had, for one thing, a wonderfully sensitive awareness of incongruities. In its serious and more usual form, it was what Arthur Mizener has described as Fitzgerald's perception of "the queerness and, occasionally, the miracle" of human experience. "For this sense of experience," Mizener observes, "Hollywood provided him with an almost perfect instance," a point he illustrates persuasively from *The Last Tycoon,* citing the freakish earthquake scene at the studios, the incident where the secretary of Cecilia's father tumbles naked out of the office closet, the love-making between Kathleen and Stahr in the latter's strangely half-real, half-finished house, and similar details. To Mizener's observation should be added another: that a number of these details are also grotesque. After he had worked his way through those earliest, thickest tangles of autobiography and sentimentality, Fitzgerald began to exercise his talent for discerning the comic in the horrible. Some instances are merely frivolous, as is the story of the Englishman in *Tender is the Night* who was shot through his identification card. Others have their relevance to the novel, as when we learn of Anthony Patch's grandfather that "The span of his seventy-five years had acted as a magic bellows—the first quarter-century had blown him full with life, and the last had sucked it all back," and so on through a memorable paragraph. Fitzgerald bent the grotesque toward humor, as a rule, but in *The Last Tycoon* nearly always gave it serious weight too. The naked, suffocating secretary should probably shock someone more than she does, but elsewhere the novelist puts such anomalies to better use. Of countless other examples in this final novel, let me mention just one—the description of Mr. Schwartz as "obviously a man to whom something had happened. Meeting him was like encountering a friend who has been in a fist fight or collision, and got flattened. You stare at your friend and say: 'What happened to you?' And he answers something unintelligible through broken teeth and swollen lips. He can't even tell you about it." The comparison does tell us about Hollywood's impact on Mr. Schwartz, which is the author's intention here, and by extension about Hollywood itself. For the incongruities of that city, the grotesque is an ideal literary medium.

Very much like D. H. Lawrence, moreover, whose work he knew and sometimes appears to echo in a lower key, Fitzgerald was both repelled and attracted by individuals who lacked emotions, worshiped abstractions and pursued things, more particularly women with these qualities. Beatrice Blaine speaks for the author, apparently, in her objection to "American women, especially the floating population of ex-Westerners," which includes nearly all the characters in his novels. " 'They have accents, my dear,' she told Amory, 'not Southern accents or Boston accents, not an accent attached to any locality, just an accent. . . .' " They drift, they have affectations;

or they practice deceptions. " 'She ought to be in the cinema,' " protests Frau Gregorovius of Nicole's pretentions to illness—" 'that's where all American women would be happy.' " To cherish appearances, to live vicariously, to exist as it were on celluloid is the nature of Fitzgerald's females, and his portraits of Rosemary and Nicole, or of such minor figures as Stella in the story "Crazy Sunday," show how well his Hollywood experiences furthered a knowledge of the type running back through Jordan Baker, Daisy, and Gloria. The only important woman character in *The Last Tycoon,* Cecilia, is too submerged in her role as narrator to be identified clearly, but the male who dominates the novel is the last and most fully drawn of the heroes who touch passion cautiously. Monroe Stahr, the Hollywood colossus, "had grown up dead cold."

In these respects and degrees, Fitzgerald had come to possess Hollywood. The pathos of his career is that Hollywood had too long possessed him. Even before his first journey West, even before he wrote Maxwell Perkins from France that if the sales of *Gatsby* were not high enough to keep him from hackwork he would "quit, come home, go to Hollywood and learn the movie business," before he had watched *Ben Hur* in Rome or received his first offers from movie agents, he had given himself too fully to the affections promoted in the great Western demiopolis. Cecilia Brady admits to herself that " 'some of my more romantic ideas actually stemmed from pictures' " and adds, " 'It's more than possible that some of the pictures which Stahr himself conceived had shaped me into what I was.' " The pictures could not have shaped Cecilia's creator so entirely, but the evidence from his fiction alone tells with what remarkable constancy over twenty years he had them in mind, beginning in "The Ice Palace" with an allusion to a "moving-picture sunset" (in 1920!) right through to the work of his last days. The ideals that sparked his imagination swarmed everywhere in American life, as we know, but particularly in its cities—bright talk, perennial youth, clothes, money, alcohol, power, easy emotions, and a consciousness of one's public. Of these ideals Hollywood quickly became (once the studios moved out there into the sun) both hot-house and pre-emptive symbol. The most sincere thing Rosemary says to Dick Diver is " 'Oh, we're such *actors*!' " Only in the scene itself does the exclamation seem abrupt; the rest of the novel, and of Fitzgerald's fiction, has prepared us for it. (Even Rosemary's declaration rings false, since the author has repeated it from an earlier story—as it happens from "Magnetism," the tale of Hollywood.) The note of pretense is heard throughout his fiction. The postures which his characters adopt are, like those of Anthony Patch in his bathroom, among their primary attributes.

Of course Fitzgerald stood outside their posturings—but how far? In his case this is a fundamental question, and the fact that it is difficult to answer furnishes a partial judgment on his work. When Monsignor Darcy tells Amory, " 'for you not posing may be the biggest pose of all,' " we are inclined to apply the diagnosis equally to Amory, the other characters, and the novelist. Fitzgerald's stylistic fabrications, particularly his gilt metaphors and relentless epigrams, contribute heavily to one's impression of an inspired counterfeiter at work. It hardly surprises us to learn that he built up a collection of "Bright Clippings" and other jewels, slipping them when he could into this or that setting. "The self-consciousness of Fitzgerald is a barrier which we are never able to pierce," remarked Heywood Broun of *This Side of Paradise*. "He sees himself constantly not as a human being, but as a man in a novel or in a play. Every move is a picture and there is a camera man behind each tree." Broun's confusion here of author with characters was fully justified.

The creation of Nick Carraway changed the contours of this fictional world. Nick is, as he describes himself, "one of the few honest people that I have ever known" and so provides a vantage-point for judgment of the less honest people around him on Long Island. Quite apart from structural and other superiorities of *The Great Gatsby* over its predecessors, Nick's presence raises this novel at least two planes above them: he supplies a firm standard by which the other characters' behavior may be evaluated, and he looks through manners into morals. Glancing back from *Gatsby* to the earlier novels, we see how harmless the misdemeanors there had been—adolescent boastings, flirtations, and ambitions in the first novel, the dissemblings of weak-willed youth in the next. But now the offenses are serious. In Daisy and Tom, Jordan Baker, Myrtle Wilson, and (though more ambiguously) in Gatsby live calculated dishonesty, deep fakery, and a terrible egoism that end in spiritual *malaise* and murder. Their evasions pass beyond children's play into matters of conduct; Tom's relationship with Myrtle has consequences. In the "carelessness" of the rich, Fitzgerald had suddenly recognized how intertwined manners may be with morals—an insight with which Henry James had had the better fortune to have begun his career—and he developed that theme with a spare magnificence that gave *Gatsby* its real distinction. This once he perceived, through Nick, the depravities of the glittering life even while its magic held. His stylistic splendor and epigrammatic wisdom no longer seemed out of place; he had grown up to them.

But then he faltered. In his art, as in his life, he had gazed at the meretricious city too long. Following *Gatsby* came his wisest stories, "The Rich Boy" in 1926, "Babylon Revisited" in 1931. Portions of *Tender is the Night* have a sadly mature kind of disillusion and a more involved knowledge than his other novels display of the way personal relationships glow and fade, but its wisdom reposes in the pieces rather than in the whole. And while *The Last Tycoon* exhibits the sudden clarity of a death-bed vision, whether a few more months would have enabled him to behold the rest of that vision remains conjectural. His synopsis for the re-

mainder of the novel leans back into plot in a manner unpromising for Fitzgerald's lyrical talent, as though the very
intimacy with the studios that permitted him to witness the
realities of Hollywood also deprived him of the detachment
or discipline or self-assurance necessary to exhibit them in
their depth or entirety. If so, it was a fate he shared in some
measure with writers as different as Nathanael West and
Norman Mailer, whose hopes to capture that enfabled city
for their art were queerly baffled once they entered the plati-
num gates. As it turned out, Fitzgerald had long before delivered hostages not to Fortune but to a fortune, and they
were never returned.

On more than one occasion early in his career, Fitzgerald
had expressed admiration for Dreiser. As city novelists they
bear interesting resemblances, but how deceptive these can
prove is shown in a passage from *The Beautiful and Damned*.
Anthony Patch, trying out as a bond salesman, cannot get interested in "the romance of finance." Unlike Clyde Griffiths,
whose ambitions leap when he enters a big company, and
totally unlike the financial genius Frank Cowperwood, Anthony quite fails to work up any enthusiasm for making
money. In Dreiser's city, the mansions of the rich stir his
heroes profoundly to dreams of wealth, love, beauty, and
independence, but to Anthony the Frick and Carnegie mansions on Fifth Avenue represent only—"an incomprehensi-
ble goal." In this as in so much else, Anthony speaks for
Fitzgerald, as we see from the retrospective essay "My Lost
City," written in 1932 though not published until 1945 (in
The Crack-up). There, recalling his own attitude in the
late 'twenties toward sections of New York that had once
meant something to him, he names Greenwich Village,
Washington Square, Murray Hill, and the Fifth Avenue
châteaux as having "disappeared, or become unexpressive
of anything." His thesis is that New York had gradually
been "lost" to him, although the essay reveals that his place
in the city, and his wife's, had always been "precarious."

The loss he felt was of the initial enchantment, with "the ferry boat moving softly from the Jersey shore at dawn," when he was "gaping" and "dazzled," when New York "had all the iridescence of the beginning of the world." At first the city had given him three symbols: the ferry, a beautiful girl, and a Princetonian bachelor's apartment (belonging to Edmund Wilson and looking very much like Anthony Patch's). These stood respectively for "triumph . . . romance . . . mellow monasticism," and in time they all slipped away from him. But as his close friend Wilson observed of him and of his New York characters in 1924, none of them convince us that they *belong* to that particular city. And they do not. Ferry, girl, and apartment—attractive, easily replaceable, and not in the least expressive of suffering or of an inescapable fate. They do not belong to Dreiser's city, in short, but to the city of mirrors.

Fitzgerald says in the same essay—drawing his example from a visit to the D. W. Griffith studio on Long Island— that "the world of the picture actors was like our own in that it was in New York and not of it. It had little sense of itself and no center: when I first met Dorothy Gish I had the feeling that we were both standing on the North Pole and it was snowing." To this he adds, "Since then they have found a home but it was not destined to be New York." The remark sounds wistful and regretful, coming as it does from a writer who surely knew by then that the only city in any sense *his* was no less a "splendid mirage" than the white-towered metropolis across the Hudson River toward which he once thought he was moving.

VII

Two Cities

WILLIAM CARLOS WILLIAMS

A poet the depths of whose candor we are still sounding, William Carlos Williams once confessed of the city beyond the river,

> For years I've been tormented by
> that miracle, the buildings all lit up—
>
> unable to say anything much to the point
> though it is the major sight
>
> of this region.

This confession is from "The Flower," one of his more difficult poems of moderate length. That Williams did write superior poems shorter than *Paterson* but longer than an image or two should hardly require saying a half-century and more after he began to publish, yet it does. His long-standing reputation as an entrenched imagist, then as a note-taker (hurriedly between patients) on small-town New Jersey folkways, continues to slow our unearthing of whatever gold his poetry may yet conceal: cunning within poems, or themes sustained over many decades. Shadowed for so long by Pound, Eliot, and Frost, he seems to have been easier for us to manage under all the early, once-tentative categories than to keep re-examining. If we return to some of these categories, as we probably shall, it should be after looking afresh at how deep and how far he really did go.

One begins or ends with *Paterson,* almost inevitably, and because *Paterson* is so expressly a city poem of some order, we may center our inquiry on what order of city it is and on what our conclusions reveal about the poem as a whole. An inquiry thus limited may have the incidental virtue of inviting new approaches to this elusive work. Most criticism to date has treated *Paterson* as illustrative—of Williams' eccentric prosody, of his reiterated principle "No ideas but in things," or of the American environment. There is something to be gained by this overhead view, as Glauco Cambon's recent essay (in *The Inclusive Flame*) makes evident. But Cambon's reading is the best we have chiefly because he also interprets the poem sensitively on its own terms and in the context of comparable literary works. Before we can have a still more inclusive study, we must back off and come at *Paterson* again from yet other directions.

If we ask what else Williams wrote on the city, we find a number of poems—not on Paterson but on New York. Scattered over some twenty-five years, these display a view of that metropolis much less varied but more intense than Whitman's from across the farther river seven or eight decades before. "The Flower," a piece from the early 1930s, shows most interestingly the character and source of this intensity. With the imagists' ostensible randomness, the speaker—an undisguised Williams—thinks of one image after another in the world about him, in turn a flower petal, city towers and bridge stanchions, places nearby in his town, a newspaper photograph, a nude woman. Gradually a central image emerges: the generalized nameless "flower." Half-buried under more vivid details, this flower is a conceit of the Brobdingnagian sort Williams employed from time to time, most boldly in *Paterson*—gigantic, a trifle fantastic, and highly arbitrary. The blossom grows (here we must consult the doctor's biography) somewhere in New Jersey; its four petals extend respectively to the towers and bridges of Manhattan, the proximate Jersey town, San Diego, and Puerto Rico. (The plant is outrageously lopsided: no objective correlative *here!*) Though the allusion to Puerto Rico shades off into autobiographical obscurity and the San Diego petal is even darker, the point of the metaphor is clear. The flower is the speaker's memory of past experience. He can still possess this past, but only through his imagination.

The theme appears mainly in the city imagery and the poet's explicit comments upon it. The occasion of the poem is the building of a great bridge:

> It is the city,
> approaching over the river. Nothing
>
> of it is mine, but visibly
> for all that it is petal of a flower—my own.

The speaker imagines other petals, then—as the "heart" of the flower "(the stamens, pistil, etc.)"—

> a naked woman, about 38, just
>
> out of bed, worth looking at both for
> her body and her mind and what she has seen
>
> and done. She it was put me straight
> about the city when I said, It
>
> makes me ill to see them run up
> a new bridge like that in a few months
>
> and I can't find time even to get
> a book written. They have the power,

> that's all, she replied. That's what you all
> want. If you can't get it, acknowledge
>
> at least what it is.

That the city represents power, its lights "the blaze of a
power/in which I have not the least part," is a truth the
speaker is forced to recognize. Not quite didactic, the poem
does by implication prescribe conduct: better to relinquish
what lies beyond your grasp and live with what you have.
This counsel of restraint, however, falls from the lips of a
disturbingly sensual woman. She distracts; but then the
poem abounds in distractions—stray thoughts of a black dog
with yellow legs eating from a garbage barrel, of the science,
philosophy, and religion he had (presumably) once been
taught, of Madame Lenine, of New Yorkers in California,
of his mother's experiences as a child. Of all these, the greatest distraction is the city, blazoning a material power the
writer cannot have. His fanciful "plan" in the closing lines
—to treat the sick by pressing buttons—is but a lament for
the same lack and a plainer announcement of the poem's
real subject: the artist's predicament in society.

This is the subject which all of Williams' New York poems
embrace. Because that city did torment him, he wrote about
it feelingly, ambiguously, and well; and because it was easy
for him to see its particular attractions and seductions in
terms of his own difficulties as a writer, first as a busy young
doctor in Manhattan hospitals and then as a still busier prac-
titioner in Rutherford snatching minutes and week-end
hours for verse, the metropolis became a convenient symbol
of the artist's social dilemma. It was his own dilemma and it
was New York, but he generalized both to some degree in
his poems. Although he says in "The Flower" of his intention there, "This/is no more a romance than an allegory,"
actually it was something of both. His tone there, as in most
of his work, is matter-of-fact, a trifle understated, quizzical,
laconic; and yet his concern with the suffering artist's plight,

viewed against the backdrop of either the American twenties or the early nineteenth century, has decidedly romantic elements, and for Williams both city and writer took on somewhat allegorical roles in this melodrama of art.

The poet's first major use of the metropolis in his poetry was for exactly the same end. "To a Friend Concerning Several Ladies" from *Sour Grapes* (1921) contrasts the speaker's commonplace desire for flowers, conversation, and poem-writing with the disruptive desires that women induce in him, passions identified with an unnamed but presumptive New York. Here Williams introduces the theme of the writer's dilemma. A woman's letter or look "comes between" the writer and his usual inclinations,

> so that I am confused, twisted
> four ways and—left flat,
> unable to lift the food to
> my own mouth. . . .

If he does not heed the invitation to "Come!/and come! and come!" to the city he is left "stale," but if he goes he disgusts himself:

> I must be
> steaming with love, colored
> like a flamingo. For what?
> To have legs and a silly head
> and to smell, pah! like a flamingo
> that soils its own feathers behind.
> Must I go home filled
> with a bad poem?

And yet "there is/no good in the world except out of a woman. . . ." The quandary of the self-obsessed artist, thus tempted and uncertain, is set forth in these lines:

> I have watched
> the city from a distance at night

> and wondered why I wrote no poem.
> Come! yes,
> the city is ablaze for you
> and you stand and look at it.

Again, as in "The Flower," the city represents a power over experience the artist both craves and scorns, his regard for which distresses him either way. The value of sensual experience affirmed in the later poem is also affirmed in this one, though in its more narrowly sexual aspects and as a waste of spirit for the artist. Here the city occupies its ancient site as the locus of sexual temptation, and there are overtones in the poem of the seduced provincial. "Clean is he alone"—goes another poem of the same period—"after whom stream/the broken pieces of the city—/flying apart at his approaches. . . ." This pair of surrealist images (from a poem on sexual passion in a city hospital, probably in Manhattan) suggests in a minor way a similar incompatibility between the metropolis and the pure life.

The element of narrative largely implicit in "The Flower" and "To a Friend" is expanded in a longer poem of the 'thirties, "Perpetuum Mobile: The City." A work of rhythmic virtuosity and a certain opaqueness, it hangs several of the earlier city motifs on a pilgrimage

> of love
> and of
> desire—

that a man and woman make to the city. Probably they are husband and wife, though one cannot be certain; in any case their destinies are joined in the same longing and the same journey. Their dreams, separate but "fused in the night," open the poem and their farewell to the city ends it. At the beginning theirs is

> A dream
> a little false

> toward which
>   now
> we stand
>   and stare
> transfixed—
>
> All at once
>   in the east
> rising!
>
>   All white!

Spectacular in their dream and at night, when "it wakes/
On the black/sky," the city beckons irresistibly. Perhaps
actually or perhaps only in their dream at last the pair
"break/through/and go there." The nature of their journey
is ambiguous. It involves in some mixture passion ("There
is no end/to desire") and art ("We batter at our/unsatis-
factory/brilliance"), but whether the passion that leads them
to the city is meant to further the artist's work or to sub-
stitute for it remains in doubt. Both readings apply.

There follow—in what is in effect the second section of
the poem—harsh glimpses of city life and death, mostly
violent. Two men armed with automatics, seemingly armored-
truck guards, rob a bank; a man's (a Negro's?) appearance
and sex are violated as long hair is tied onto the "kinky wool"
of his "whorish head"; someone is

> Dragged
>   insensible
> upon his face
> by the lines—
>
> —a running horse
>
>   For love.

> Their eyes
>   blown out—
>   —for love, for love!

Now the pace, after fifty clipped lines of quickly changing
rhythms, changes again—to the slow crawl of the mailman's
platitudinous motto ("Neither the rain/Nor the storm—"),
which Williams deftly rescues from its triteness by one more
repetition of the exclamatory "for love!" All the violence
has been *for love!* Like the two pilgrims' trek to the city, the
violence itself has sprung from love and desire.

To the violent in Williams' city is joined the excremental.
While above-ground city dwellers are "Guzzling/the creamy
foods," beneath them the waste fat and old vegetables are

> chucked down
>   a chute
>   the foulest
>   sink in the world—

and out through this sewer goes the garbage to sea, where
an eel fattens itself in the water pipe. The garbage at sea is
said to be "like weed/that held back/the pristine ships"—
possibly the ships of Columbus, or of the first settlers, who
were thus prevented from touching the fair New World. If
so, the simile repeats an idea introduced early in the poem,
that the city represents a corrupting of some earlier, innocent, perhaps pastoral vision. The travelers' is a "false
dream": the city is the ideal gone bad, illusion.

What remains attractive in the poem is nature. The city
fouls the sea, as in other poems Williams speaks of its foul-
ing the rivers, but left alone nature can be seen in its ideal
aspects. The garb in which the city first luminously appears
to the dreamers of "Perpetuum Mobile" is that of the spring-
time locust, shad, and magnolia, budding and blossoming;
and the couple's departure finds them viewing the city again,
in the reluctant aftermath of disillusion, through vivid image-

ry of stars, clouds, and moon. Nature is the end, as it was
the beginning: the "hard grey" of the city, its "iron reason/
and stone," fades "in a wall of/rain. . . ." We are left to
infer that nature, or a natural life, is a cleanly preferable
alternative—a view that does not sound much like the tough-
grained realist we elsewhere know Williams to be. It both
does and does not. There are no sermons in brooks, if there
ever were, he maintains in one mood, as in this opening
stanza from "Raleigh Was Right":

> We cannot go to the country
> for the country will bring us
>   no peace
> What can the small violets tell us
> that grow on furry stems in
> the long grass among lance shaped
>   leaves?

Emerson was wrong. But Williams had other moods, as
when, admiring a rotten apple, he manages to represent it
as an ideal form:

> O lovely apple!
> beautifully and completely
>   rotten,
> hardly a contour marred—
>
>   perhaps a little
> shrivelled at the top but that
>   aside perfect
> in every detail! . . .

This poem is entitled "Perfection." Williams was not finely
consistent in such matters, nor would he have cared to be. In
its main features, though, his rural sympathies remained a
stable quantity in his verse. ("I was always a country boy,"
he remarked to Edith Heal, "felt myself a country boy. To
me the countryside was a real world but nonetheless a poetic

world. I have always had a feeling of identity with nature, but not assertive. . . .") There are "draining places," he says in a trenchant bit of light verse from the 1940s, "from which New York/is dignified, created," and the kinds of human activity and botanical detail he selects from these outlying rural places provide a concise inventory of qualities Williams found lacking in the city:

> A church in New Hampshire
> built by its pastor
> from his own wood lot. One
> black (of course, red)
> rose; a fat old woman backing
> through a screen door. Two,
> from the armpits
> down, contrasting in bed,
> breathless; a letter from
> a ship; leaves filling,
> making, a tree (but
> wait) not just leaves,
> leaves of one design that
> make a certain design,
> no two alike, not like
> the locust either, next in line,
> nor the Rose of Sharon, in
> the pod-stage, near it—a
> tree! Imagine it! Pears
> philosophically hard. Nor
> thought that is from
> branches on a root, from
> an acid soil, with scant
> grass about the bole
> where it breaks through.

The indigenous, the self-reliant, the natural, the spontaneous, the comic, the passionate, the wonderful, the regenerative, the unique, the concrete, the fundamental, the tilled—the list is a peculiarly American blend, exposing some of Williams' own roots in traditions shared by Cummings and Whitman but running most directly back to Emerson and Thoreau. His ire had been aroused by two groups of people in New York, the conformist "herd" and avant-garde writers. Part lyric, part ridicule, "A Place (Any Place) to Transcend All Places" assumes that the artist of individuality and sense will despise both groups. "New York is built of/such grass and weeds. . . ." By the closing stanza (having rotted?), the grass and weeds have become "Obscene and/abstract as excrement," good for growing lettuce, "if you/like lettuce."

A topical piece, its hostility toward the city nevertheless is of a kind we meet in his deeper poems, a hostility that flows from the same anxieties. The historian of imaginary cities will detect traces in Williams' mind of a stereotyped metropolis, but the more germane feature for an understanding of this particular poet is his habit of seeing it as a threat to the writer, which is to say himself. To Williams, the city is meaningful *primarily* in its relationship to the artist, and he perceives that relationship for the most part in terms of power, harassment, and disillusion. We fail to notice this side of Williams —to my knowledge, no one has mentioned it—because it is such a quiet controlled little anxiety, not at all like the outbursts of a Swift; but its essentials resemble those animating much of *Gulliver's Travels,* including the symptomatic interest in violent and excremental imagery.

A gauge of Williams' preoccupation with this subject and of his ability to turn it toward a literary end is an admirable poem of the 1920s, "A Morning Imagination of Russia." Framed as an interior monologue by a Soviet intellectual in the post-Revolutionary era, it is a distinctly symbolic poem, its symbols drawn principally from the city and nature. In it the poet contrasts present with past (Czarist, certainly) and behind that past still another one. The immediate, pre-Revolutionary past is a time of cities. The present and the very remote past are times when cities did not enter significantly into a man's life. The difference is—"everything."

> Cities are full of light, fine clothes
> delicacies for the table, variety,
> novelty—fashion: all spent for this.
> Never to be like that again:
> the frame that was.

Money and other possessions have left the nation (with White Russian *émigrés,* no doubt), a kind of riches no longer desirable. Now wealth is inner, "scattered wealth," to be found only "close to his heart." We have heard the theme in the New York verses: the city is a barrier to one's encounter with experience. Now, as this lone Russian faced his new life,

> There were no cities
> between him and his desires
> his hatreds and his loves were without walls
> without rooms, without elevators
> without files, delays of veiled murderers
> muffled thieves, the tailings of
> tedious, dead pavements, the walls
> against desire save only for him who can pay
> high, there were no cities. . . .

With cities have disappeared the coercions of power, secret violence.

Replacing them is a life close to the earth and sky, in which a man tends his own fire, picks his own herbs, and need not shave in the morning to assume his duties as a local magistrate. Or—as a poet? It could almost be either, so incidental is the man's specific vocation. He could stand, easily, as surrogate for the artist, so cut off from experience he has been as Williams' American writer is, so freed now—impediments having vanished—to take up his work. But what the Soviet intellectual finds is that experience crawls with uncertainties:

When the sun rose it rose in his heart
It bathed the red cold world of
the dawn so that the chill was his own. . . .

The world was himself, these were
his own eyes that were seeing, his own mind
that was straining to comprehend, his own
hands that would be touching other hands
These were his own!
His own, feeble, uncertain.

"We have little now," thinks the magistrate, "but/we have
that." Read as evidence of Williams' Russian sympathies, the
lines sound romantically hopeful; as a pronouncement of the
liberated artist, they sound tremulous. In the face of experience, directly confronted, his powers are *feeble, uncertain.*
What he has is "touch. The eyes and the ears/down on it.
Close." But will touch, sight, and hearing suffice?

If we take these lines as merely another phrasing of Williams' empiricism, then Yes, the senses will suffice: all
knowledge derives from experience, ideas rise from things.
Paterson, however, suggests what his New York poems suggest—that his empirical doctrine voices a fear as radically
as it describes a poetic practice, that Williams sensed or
realized how prone he was to an extreme subjectivity, to
denying the reality of the external world, to crying (as he
does in "The Host") *Only the imagination/is real!* Indeed,
a distinguishing characteristic of his wonderfully absorbing
long poem seems to me exactly the reverse of one commonly
ascribed to it and to his poetry generally. In conception and
execution, *Paterson* displays an astonishing bias toward ideas
over things, the abstract over the concrete, mind over the ex-
periential. While Williams mistrusts and berates the "divorce" of language from fact—the peril of this separation is
his leading argument—his poem itself discloses precisely this
split between the poet's own sensibility and the world.

To see the way this split appears in his work, we may fix our sights on the 'city' in *Paterson*, Williams' second city.

"I conceived the whole of *Paterson* at one stroke," the poet told Henry Wells in 1955, "and wrote it down—as it appears at the beginning of the poem." That introductory "Argument" is actually a statement of the underlying conception: "that a man in himself is a city, beginning, seeking, achieving and concluding his life in ways which the various aspects of a city may embody—if imaginatively conceived—any city, all the details of which may be made to voice his most intimate convictions." The phrase "may be made" has significance, first of all as indicating Williams' starting-point in the man's (Mr. Paterson's) consciousness, rather than in the place (Paterson, New Jersey). The place was thought of as serving *secondarily,* and that is what it does in the poem as written. A substantial difficulty is that the city of Paterson never emerges in sufficient richness of detail to persuade us of its reality. All we learn from the entire five books is that "Paterson lies in the valley under the Passaic Falls," that the river from the Falls runs some distance along one edge of the city, that the houses of the city have "blank faces" and the trees there are "bent, forked . . . split, furrowed, creased, mottled, stained," that there are church spires and tall "pearl-grey" office buildings in the city, that there are suburbs in which (?) stand red-brick buildings having "Tenement windows, sharp edged, in which/no face is seen —though curtainless, into/which no more than birds and insects look or/the moon stares," that it has or has had factories, some for silk, that it has "garbage on the curbs" and "spreading slums." These details are found in the verse portions. Most of the interspersed prose passages contain historical material—from old newspaper clippings, anecdotes, local chronicles—and while this material does resurrect eighteenth- and nineteenth-century Paterson, and fits into the thematic network of the poem, for this reader, at least, not one but two different Patersons emerge, one present and one past, one suggestive and the other severely prosaic. Although they are certainly intended to fuse, to show the interpenetration of epochs and of layers of experience in the protagonist's (Mr. Paterson's) mind, they seldom do so. This is partly because the ancient Paterson is largely confined to the prose, the other to the verse, and also because the older town is presented almost entirely through realistic devices (the newspaper clippings, etc.) whereas the contemporary city is, as I have indicated, hardly concrete at all. Williams' belief that prose and verse ought not to be sharply differentiated has obvious critical merits, but a reader nonetheless responds to familiar cues on the printed page and so separates the two as he proceeds. The result for *Paterson* is an unfortunate loss in imaginative coherence.

Here one may object that *of course* we are not told much about the present-day Paterson, that it is a symbolic city, as Eliot's was in "Prufrock" or the "Preludes," or as Williams' New York was. That Paterson is meant to be symbolic is indeed part of the point, to appreciate which it is first necessary to rid ourselves of the specious notion of Williams' everlasting objectivism. The rest of the point is that, granting a symbolic intent, Paterson is simply too vaporous to work well as symbol, as allegory, or even as analogy. Here and there, as in the lines on tenement windows, it functions magically as metaphor; but one must strain to speak of a broadly symbolic city in the poem as a whole. From the fifty-four lines of Eliot's "Preludes" one learns almost as much about a poet's 'city' as from any one Book of *Paterson,* and nearly all of this detail is put to work. Without the withered leaves, the broken blinds and chimney-pots, the sparrows in the gutters and all the rest, there would be no poem; but oddly enough that could not be said of *Paterson.* Books Three and Four are so tenuously located in time and space, furthermore, that they could be thought to repose almost any time and anywhere. (One blinks to hear from Sister M. Bernetta Quinn that the Library in Book Three is "probably the Danforth Memorial Library at the corner of SE Broadway and Auburn in Paterson.") But if the temporal and geographical matter so little, one wonders, then why emphasize as Williams does the parallels between the city and Mr. Paterson—or the notion that the city "may embody" the man's four stages of life? (Book Five, we recall, was an afterthought.) The man's *beginning, seeking, achieving,* and *concluding* are difficult enough to identify, either book-by-book or as interwoven phases of his experience, and those of the city seem to me nearly impossible.

To think in such terms—that is, to try to establish the city and the hero *clearly* in the poet's announced plan—is thus to lay bare probable sources of dissatisfaction with the poem that readers have hitherto only felt. Among modern writers known to Williams, it was Joyce who most notably exploited correspondences in topography and character, who painstakingly forced the city to lend itself to his symbolic scheme. Though the plan of Paterson owes much to *Finnegans Wake,* however—Williams has spoken of reading *Ulysses* at the time the plan "dawned on me"—his notion of a city that is seeking and achieving somehow failed to grow into a sustained or persuasive structure for the poem. It seems to have served Williams as an inspirational source, but as an operative idea in the various books it is almost an excrescence.

What the city of Paterson contributes principally to the poem is a part of itself—its lower classes. The city comes most alive through them, the epic comes most alive, through "the working classes," the Great Beast (Hamilton's epithet, heard periodically throughout the sections), creatures of the factories and churches who inhabit the slums and fill the Park on Sundays. We meet these coarsely sensual males and females, their "Minds beaten thin/by waste," mainly in Book Two, and it is there that Williams develops the theme of a "debased city." These laborers and their consorts *are* the Debased City; they represent it primarily. How much more earnestly Williams takes them than he does other elements of the city of Paterson may be felt in differences of tone be-

tween Book Two and Book Three, or in the more forceful
imagery with which he presents the proletarians:

> . . . the ravished park, torn by
> the wild workers' children tearing up the grass,
> kicking, screaming. . . .

> . . . their mouths eating and kissing,
> spitting and sucking. . . .

>   An incredible
> clumsiness of address,
> senseless rapes—caught on hands and knees
> scrubbing a greasy corridor; the blood
> boiling as though in a vat. . . .

> . . . the ugly legs of the young girls,
> pistons too powerful for delicacy!
> the men's arms, red, used to heat and cold,
> to toss quartered beeves. . . .

And in this Sunday in the Park of the second book there is the
intermittent narrative of the beer-drinking, butt-smoking
couple sexually engaged, animalistically, half-publicly. "It
is all for/pleasure. . . ." In the pleasure park all is debased—
love into sexual boredom, mind into "pitiful thoughts,"
speech into inarticulateness, creativity into idling and loiter-
ing, healthy bodies into deformities, history into the purely
contemporaneous, culture into a vulgar dance, time into
death, religion into a pitchman's Evangelism enacted for an
indifferent crowd near the urinals.

The implied values are so fully ours who read this poem
that it is easy to overlook two things about them: that they
are somewhat more important to the poet than the human individuals who have degraded them, and that they are by and
large the values of an artist. The first of these assertions
would take a lengthy analysis of *Paterson* to demonstrate, but

its truth may be suggested by the disparaging tone and the generality with which Williams usually presents the factory workers. He does speak of them in one passage as "those poor souls" with "nothing else in the world, save that church, between them and eternal stony, ungrateful and unpromising dirt they lived by," and that "Cash is mulct of them that others may live/secure/. . . and knowledge restricted./An orchestral dullness overlays their world. . . ." But Hamilton's epithet of the Great Beast, with its heavily pejorative overtones, is the one that Williams seems most content with. Sympathetic or not, the poet stands apart from these degenerate spirits; like the Jackson Whites of this poem and others, they interest him insofar as they *are* degenerate. We see them not as individuals but as symptoms of a cultural disease.

Here the New York poems help us perceive what we might otherwise ignore: that the pathology of this disease is given us by the artist. Mr. Paterson is a writer, he interprets the park scene for us, and almost everything he encounters in his ramble there disturbs him. He too suffers the divorce of language from life, Williams emphasizes, but because he liberally identifies his hero with himself, we may take Mr. Paterson's plaints as substantially his own. These are, once more, an expression of fear for the artist's world—for love, mind, speech, creativity, health, history, culture, time, and belief. As projections of this anxiety, the metropolis and the provincial city become one: they are Society, the Outer World, Reality threatening the Artistic Sensibility.

Solipsism is therefore both a theme and a condition of *Paterson*. Williams' longstanding fascination with the difficulties of communicating—with the "imprisoned mind," as he once called it—should be inspected more closely than it has been. When he reiterates, as he does, that only the imagination is real, we are obliged to accept that as one of his beliefs, merely setting it alongside his other, imagist's assumption that a real world exists first of all outside the imagination. With a pluralist's readiness to abide by an inconsistent metaphysics, Williams moved without visible tremors from realism to idealism, in technique from the objective to its opposite. His variety, like Cleopatra's, is at once a source of our delight and our confusion. But then he never pretended to consistency, or did not consistently pretend, so that we can seldom know when to take him at his word.

Happily for his interpreters, Williams was given to a kind of inadvertent candor. Like any poet, he can be pinned to the truth of his imagery; but he had also the habit of dropping statements in his poems that reveal more than he might have suspected. One of these disclosures reposes quietly in Book Five of *Paterson,* in scraps of a letter from Allen Ginsberg (or "A.G."). As a corrective to the common view of this poem, Ginsberg's comment is superb: "I mean to say Paterson is not a task like Milton going down to hell, it's a flower to the mind too. . . ."

It *is* a flower—a delicate blue narcissus.

VIII

Rome Sacked

W . H . AUDEN

One of the first poems in Auden's earliest important collection, the *Poems* of 1930, carries this warning:

> Think—Romans had a language in their day
> And ordered roads with it, but it had to die:
> Your culture can but leave. . . .

Several elements are to become characteristic: the admonition to his contemporaries, the double focus on modern and ancient civilizations, the singling out of language in its practical bearings on these civilizations, the assumption that history is cyclical or otherwise repetitive and historical parallels are therefore enlightening, and the ambiguously neutral attitude concerning the climax of this historical process. Auden's evolutionary and vaguely Marxian emphasis in the 1930 version of this poem shifted slightly in 1945 by his addition of a title pointing up the Eros theme ("Venus Will Now Say a Few Words"); but as Joseph Warren Beach recognized in noting the change (in *The Making of the Auden Canon*), the poem still centers on a world in decline. In this and other verse of the early thirties Auden had not yet begun to use the city distinctly as an emblem of cultural crisis. His obvious interest in city life, however, as well as the usual tone of his topical references ("this assaulted city," "policed unlucky city," "starved city"), and his generalizing, historicizing proclivities all pointed toward this symbolic end.

Moreover, the machinery that rusts on his landscapes of this period has been strewn over the countryside by a civilization pre-eminently industrial and urban:

> Smokeless chimneys, damaged bridges, rotting wharves
>   and choked canals,
> Tramlines buckled, smashed trucks lying on their side
>   across the rails;
>
> Power-stations locked, deserted, since they drew the
>   boiler fires;
> Pylons fallen or subsiding, trailing dead high-tension
>   wires. . . .
>
> Metals run
> Burnished or rusty in the sun
> From town to town. . . .

The Epilogue to *Look, Stranger!* of 1936 links these signs of a capitalist-industrial collapse directly to the city, and intimates that social failures, superficial or deep, derive not just from a class but from everyone:

> Certainly our city—with the byres of poverty down to
> The river's edge, the cathedral, the engines, the dogs;
>   Here is the cosmopolitan cooking
>   And the light alloys and the glass.
> Built by the conscious-stricken, the weapon-making,
> By us.

The phrase "conscious-stricken" leaps out. In his book *Obsessive Images,* Beach (or the typographer) misquotes it as "conscience-stricken," an error that brings us quickly to the point. The modern city is smitten by intellect rather than by a moral sense. While this notion is understandable enough, it

sits strangely with the implied objection to the weapon-
makers. Intellect brings weapons bring poverty, we must suppose—a construction that harmonizes with the anti-mechanis-
tic view of modern history Auden would later adopt. But the
connections among ideas here are extremely diagrammatic.

Nevertheless the ideas themselves are worth noticing, as
initial expressions of city themes soon to become prominent
in the poetry. Intellect, especially, plays a curious role in the
single poem of the period 1928–36 addressed squarely to
these themes. There, in the sestina eventually to be titled
"Paysage Moralisé," one Auden 'city' appears with startling
completeness. The brief analysis Beach has given this poem
holds up so well that I offer it here as our preliminary guide:

> Cities represent the ideal commonwealth, and their builders
> are to be honored. They are places of learning. The ideal is
> not fully realized and cities become starving and unhappy;
> they become dilapidated and need rebuilding. It is natural
> for their sorrowing denizens to dream of islands where
> there is dancing and greenness: they imagine lovely gods
> who come from islands and invite you to return with them
> across the water; there are always pilgrims describing these
> places of dreams. Some villagers are too apathetic in spite
> of their wretchedness to undertake the journey. Of those
> who do undertake it, many perish in the mountains, many
> but take their sorrow to other unhappy cities, many are
> drowned in the life-giving water. . . . The thing to do is
> not dream of islands but rebuild the city, restore the social
> ideal.

By focusing on certain elements to the exclusion of others,
Beach hit upon an interpretation that is—despite these ex-
clusions—still superbly right. The reason for this odd result
I shall indicate presently.

Beach is really quite wrong in one fundamental respect.
The ideal human state Auden hints of in *"Paysage Moralisé"*
is not just social; it is *at once* social and private. Beach's state-

ments about the "ideal commonwealth" and "social ideal"
denote one aspect only of this conception. Actually Auden
treats the moral and broadly political as parts of the same
whole. Two features in particular establish this relation: the
idea of sorrow and the water image. The founders of cities
were possessed of a "sorrow/That brought them desperate to
the brink of valleys." This sorrow is also ours, though
through some blindness we fail to "see its likeness" in theirs.
Sorrow is, in short, a perennial human condition, leading
some men to found cities, their descendants to suffer there.
City-dwellers dream of escape from this condition; "pilgrims" report its possibility to villagers. Both types of men
see in escape an opportunity to enjoy themselves, to know
"innocent" love, and to

> ". . . forget your sorrow,
>   The shadow cast across your lives by mountains."

But escape is illusory. There is in fact none—save by water:

It is the sorrow; shall it melt? Ah, water
Would gush, flush green these mountains and these valleys,
And we rebuild our cities, not dream of islands.

Water makes green, purifies, brings (or returns) fertility to
the "barren mountains" and "wretched valleys," and enables
men—enables us—to restore our cities. Water therefore represents some healing, enabling power that dissipates sorrow
and encourages action toward the ideal.

It represents, in Christian terms, faith. Indeed, *"Paysage
Moralisé"* makes nearly perfect sense as a Christian allegory
—more precisely, as an allegory of Christian belief conceived
historically. Briefly stated, our forefathers tried to establish
a community where divine law reigned. We should honor
their attempt and the law embodied in that community. The
founding of these "cities," however, did not guarantee their
prosperity. Our forebears, imperfect since Adam, soon
dreamed of the lost Eden or of a life given over to pleasure.

Their descendants, with the shadow of sin more visibly across their lives, have fallen into deeper errors. Some (the "moping villagers"), afflicted by gloominess (*tristitia*) or languid indifference (*acedia*), fail in their moral duties. False "pilgrims" tempt them, moreover, with visions of an earthly paradise—a pagan vision, the mortal pride and beauty of whose gods lure them to forsake their unhappy circumstances. Many, thus tempted, perish on the heights of sin; others turn toward the cities only from a lack of courage; still others drown from too swift a plunge into faith; some, overcome by guilt, make no effort of any kind. "We," of course, are one with the villagers in needing faith to "rebuild our cities."

Biblical overtones sound everywhere in the poem, from the valleys in shadow to the mountains that faith could move, from the cities built by rivers to the souls who thirst for baptismal water and who hunger. The Hopkinsian (penultimate) line of the tercet has also the effect of a Christian allusion, while the reference to pilgrims, the idea of seekers who fall by the wayside, and the emphasis on obligation all serve to recall the travail of Bunyan's erring traveler.

And yet Christian's journey to the Celestial City somehow does not quite provide an appropriate context. "Starving" cities, for one thing, suggest Auden's concern with the earthly and immediate, though possibly because we know from other work of his interest in social problems of the depression years. Then too the religious allegory seems oblique, jutting to the surface at the queer angle of an ironic "pilgrims." The idea of "*learned* cities," however, throws up the largest difficulty to a consistently religious view of the poem. As Beach felt, these cities are sympathetically presented, as visionary dreams the founders had and to whose pursuit we should return. But the ideal of learning or intellect they were to realize is, of course, markedly unchristian. We are therefore confronted with two ideal cities, one having almost everything in common with Augustine's heavenly "society of holy men and good angels," the other quite terrestrial. Following

Auden's own emphasis, near the beginning and in the concluding line of the poem, leads Beach to an understandable
emphasis on the earthly city; assuming that there must be a
thematic unity leads Monroe K. Spears (in his generally able
biography) into the cul-de-sac of fragmentary comment. But
though the discrepancies are less noticeable in this knotty
early poem than in verse to come, the two cities actually represent partially irreconcilable values—religious on the one
hand, worldly on the other.

One of these cities reappears in "Spain 1937," to be further
specified and named. A masterful exercise in the use of
classical rhetorical techniques, this poem has at its dramatic
center the vision of individuals and groups self-preoccupied
or otherwise inert, yet responsive to the summons of selfless
public duty. Calling for aid to Spain, nations invoke the
"life," the potentiality for altruistic action, in man;

And the life, if it answers at all, replies from the heart
And the eyes and the lungs, from the shops and squares of
    the city. . . .

This life is now dormant in the "Yes-man, the bar-com-
panion, the easily-duped," all found in "the corrupt heart of
the city." But it can be aroused:

"What's your proposal? To build the Just City? I will."

Spain is to be aided; but it is also an arena for moral regeneration. Spain offers, to a degree, redemptive opportunity. The
City of God has thus been transposed to earth, becoming the
"Just City." That such a conception is compatible with Augustine's *civitas Dei,* although not mentioned in the fifth-century
treatise which defines it, is made clear by the Catholic scholar
Étienne Gilson. "St. Augustine did not bequeath to his suc-
cessors an ideal of a universal human city united in view of
purely temporal ends proper to it," Gilson has stated; "but it
was enough that the City of God exist in order to inspire men
with the desire to organize the earth into a single society

made to the image and likeness of the heavenly City." The "men of our day," Gilson adds, "hope to construct a third city, which would be temporal like the earthly city, yet just in a temporal way. . . ." In the exhortation on Spain this third city stands for exactly that temporal justice. In retrospect this Just City seems also to approximate the moral community we are urged—in *"Paysage Moralisé"*—to rebuild, while Auden's growing attention to Christian orthodoxy after 1937 makes it likely that this variant of Augustine's city would turn up yet again.* It does, frequently, along with the purely secular city, the community of intellect. These two cities, considered together, help define Auden's ideals and certain problems they raise.

"In the bus to-day," the poet wrote Erika Mann Auden from Iceland in 1936, "I had a bright idea about this travel book. I brought a Byron with me to Iceland, and I suddenly thought I might write him a chatty letter in light verse about anything I could think of, Europe, literature, myself. He's the right person I think, because he was a townee, a European, and disliked Wordsworth and that kind of approach to nature, and I find that very sympathetic." The remark borders on the frivolous, as did the ensuing letters to Byron published in his (and MacNeice's) travel potpourri the next year—but with exactly the self-conscious urbanity we would expect from a precocious child born to professional middle-class parents, the English public schools, and Oxford. To be a townee was to follow Byron's muse, "because she's gay and witty,/Be-

---

* It turns up not only in later verse but also in his prose, as in this passage from *The Enchafèd Flood* (1950): "The images of the Just City, of the civilised landscape protected by the Madonna, the *'Fior, frondi, ombre, antri, onde, aure soavi'* which look at us from so many Italian paintings, and of the rose garden or island of the blessed, are lacking in Romantic literature because the Romantic writers no longer believe in their existence. What exists is the Trivial Unhappy Unjust City, the desert of the average from which the only escape is to the wild, lonely, but still vital sea." Among the interesting features of Auden's statement is the *static* quality of this one city ideal, as he conceives of it.

cause she's neither prostitute nor frump,/The daughter of a
European city,/And country houses long before the slump.
. . .'' Like Auden's story (reported in *The Dyer's Hand*)
that he prevented embarrassments with strangers on trains by
announcing his occupation as Medieval Historian, the frolic
is at least half-significant. The intellectual's proper habitat
was the city *of course*. There—where else?—was wit, honor,
lively good nature, gentlemanly tradition. There was courtesy,
culture. There was the center from which the cultivated
looked out upon the world.

But culture lived within a very small circle, in "the draw-
ing-room's civilised cry," behind the "narrow window" of a
fourth-floor room. Looking out, one saw the urban masses,
suburban lives, the bourgeois rich, routine and hedonism, the
materialistic and ordinary. In August "the people" could be
observed at their shallow amusements; "The sallow oval
faces of the city/Begot in passion or good-natured habit" took
steamers or trains, sunbathed "Beside the undiscriminating
sea," hiked to the moors, behaved childishly.

> The gulls ask for them, and to them the band
> Makes its tremendous statements. . . .

At Oxford, outside the quadrangle walls were "the shops, the
works, the whole green county/Where a cigarette comforts
the guilty and a kiss the weak;/There thousands fidget and
poke and spend their money. . . ." While inside, Success was
honored:

> Promising to the sharp sword all the glittering prizes,
> The cars, the hotels, the service, the boisterous bed,
> Then power to silence outrage with a testament. . . .

A stranger in Brussels found only "Ridges of rich apart-
ments" and "the homeless and the really humbled . . . in their
misery." While in New York,

> Faces along the bar
> Cling to their average day:

> The lights must never go out,
> The music must always play,

a customary mindlessness matched by the moral triviality of the "dense commuters" who come

> From the conservative dark
> Into the ethical life . . .
> Repeating their morning vow;
> "I *will* be true to the wife,
> I'll concentrate more on my work. . . ."

While these passages from poems of the thirties show an obvious satirical bent, their brevity shows how limited Auden's interest was in mounting satiric attacks on the common man. "The Unknown Citizen" stands almost alone as a poem directed wholly to this end, and it is a short effort indeed. What Auden's gibes at the middle and lower city classes do reveal is a marked condescension, not to say snobbish insularity. Average people are Out There—and aren't they dull, shallow, and mediocre? There is no reason not to accept as genuine Auden's intellectual sympathy with "the homeless and the really humbled," but such generalized humanitarian assertions are easily outweighed over the years by instances of polite derision.

This deep indifference to average persons, or contempt for them, must be borne in mind when we try to determine exactly what kind of community Auden would like to see realized. When he speaks of the Just City, particularly in a religious context, we may take him to mean that Christian social order in which justice prevails equally for all men. But as we have begun to perceive, he also loves a more purely secular city, based on distinctions and exclusions. What happens when these ideals meet is intimated in a poem first published in 1939, "The Capital." Though focused on a presumptively real city, the poem conveys a strong sense of what 'urban' life could be. At present the metropolis is destructive or corrupt:

Quarter of pleasures where the rich are always waiting,
Waiting expensively for miracles to happen. . . .

. . . with orchestras and glances, O, you betray us
To belief in our infinite powers; and the innocent
Unobservant offender falls in a moment
Victim to the heart's invisible furies.

In unlighted streets you hide away the appalling;
Factories where lives are made for a temporary use
Like collars* or chairs, rooms where the lonely are battered
Slowly like pebbles into fortuitous shapes.

In the second and last of five stanzas, however, it promises a
kind of rescue:

Far from your lights the outraged punitive father,
The dullness of mere obedience here is apparent. . . .

But the sky you illumine, your glow is visible far
Into the dark countryside, the enormous, the frozen. . . .

Here rural life is the wasteland. Though menacing, the city
does offer "the farmer's children" fredom from parental
coercion and the stimulation that such freedom brings. These
advantages, it should be noted, are couched not so much in
moral as in social or aesthetic terms. Lives are coerced in the
city too, but there at least one escapes from "dullness." The
advantage in liveliness hardly outweighs one's submission to
a new yoke, although the poet implies that it does. Given this
imbalance in alternatives, the poem proves neither resolved
nor clearly ambiguous. The moral issues have not been
brought into a clear relationship with the more narrowly
social ones, virtue with enlightenment.

These two spheres of conduct draw Auden's attention in-

* The collar factory provides a wonderfully apt symbol of the individual's loss of freedom in an industrial society, as Stephen Crane
(in *Maggie*) and Dreiser (in *An American Tragedy*) also recognized.

creasingly thereafter, beginning most notably with the "New Year Letter" of 1940. In that spasmodically brilliant melange of spiritual autobiography, social comment, intellectual history, topicality, philosophy, theology and what not, one cannot speak of thematic unities, even if one were so minded. Much of the poem is a thinking-aloud, in a literary sense improvised. Like all aphorists, Auden has always had trouble cementing large wholes together, so that it is almost as irrelevant to look for overriding consistencies in his themes as it is in Emerson's or Nietzsche's. Almost, but not totally; for unlike these seers, Auden has, while rejecting a perfect *ordre logique,* valued order extremely. "New Year Letter" has explicit statements on exactly this point, indeed returns repeatedly to it. The principal imagery through which he conveys the idea is that of the city—or once again, of cities, for he is still nurturing a double vision of the future.

The brief Prologue aside, the poem begins and ends topically, confessionally, with statements about the actuality of disorder and the need for order. Europe is at war; one's own life is a muddle. Against the disharmonies of events—the social catastrophes, the "hidden force" that disrupts the course of history—stand isolated areas of stability. The third stanza describes one such area:

> The very morning that the war
> Took action on the Polish floor,
> Lit up America and on
> A cottage in Long Island shone
> Where Buxtehude as we played
> One of his *passacaglias* made
> Our minds a *civitas* of sound
> Where nothing but assent was found,
> For art had set in order sense
> And feeling and intelligence,
> And from its ideal order grew
> Our local understanding too.

Art supplies order—that is a part of the argument, a part that Auden carries on fitfully for some stanzas until it dissolves into speculations on his own fate as an artist. But another part, of which the poet seems less certainly aware, rests in that Long Island cottage. Why mention the surroundings in which he heard the *passacaglias*? Because these matter to him too. The *civitas* of art accords with, doubtless requires, a *civitas* of feeling and intelligent spirits. This goodly fellowship of music appreciators may be viewed in the context of Auden's longstanding fascination with the social psychology of art, with the conditions under which it is created and received. (The succeeding stanzas of "New Year Letter," for instance, take up the relationship of art to the individual and society, then the great artists "as personalities," and Auden's own misgivings in the face of hypothetical judgments on his work by poets from Dante to Kipling.) Quite independently of that context, though, these cultivated souls are to be seen as a civil body Auden values for itself. This ideal would seem to govern the second stanza in Part III (part of the first stanza in the English edition) which otherwise looks gratuitously autobiographical:

> Warm in your house, Elizabeth,
> A week ago at the same hour
> I felt the unexpected power
> That drove our ragged egos in
> From the dead-ends of greed and sin
> To sit down at the wedding feast,
> Put shining garments on the least,
> Arranged us so that each and all,
> The erotic and the logical,
> Each felt the *placement* to be such
> That he was honored overmuch,
> And Schubert sang and Mozart played
> And Gluck and food and friendship made
> Our privileged community

> That real republic which must be
> The State all politicians claim,
> Even the worst, to be their aim.

The overtones of a mixed uneasiness and pride in this social
elite are strengthened by the quotation from Flaubert which
Auden appends as a note to the phrase "Our privileged community": " 'Don't let's pity ourselves. We are the privileged.
Our minds are lit by gas. There are so many people who are
shivering in attics without even candles.' "

In a convulsed world, then, the gas-lit community provides
a certain necessary order. But that order seems self-enclosed,
quite cut off from the Just City to which men were summoned
in "Spain 1937." Another passage in Part III of the "Letter"
supplies, in effect, a commentary on that problem. Declaring
his bewilderment midst all the "calls to conscience" in the
desperate world around him, the poet says that we must not
trust demagogues or nationalist politicians: "We can at least
serve other ends." The ends he names are these:

> We . . .
> Can love the *polis* of our friends
> And pray that loyalty may come
> To serve mankind's *imperium.*

Rationally or imaginatively there is the gap to be bridged—
between the smaller and larger communities, private and
public loyalties, the city of privileged gentlefolk and the city
of mankind. The gap appears a chasm. How do we move
from the narrower to the broader community? One cannot
say, Auden implies; one can only pray that the first loyalty
will lead to the second. In the line immediately following that
last quoted above, Auden himself raises the question of
means: "But why and where and when and how?" It is
significant that he never answers that question, in this poem
or another.

Between the two cities he would like to see established the

canals are in fact choked, the rails rusted. But that Auden thinks communication entirely possible is made evident in many lines from this and later years, as in these from "New Year Letter":

> The future which confronts us has
> No likeness to that age when, as
> Rome's huggermugger unity
> Was slowly knocked to pieces by
> The uncoördinated blows
> Of artless and barbaric foes,
> The stressed and rhyming measures rose;
> The cities we abandon fall
> To nothing primitive at all;
> This lust in action to destroy
> Is not the pure instinctive joy
> Of animals, but the refined
> Creation of machines and mind.
> We face our self-created choice*
> As out of Europe comes a voice,
> A theologian who denies
> What more than twenty centuries
> Of Europe have assumed to be
> The basis of civility. . . .

The idea of *civility* appears beautifully to link Auden's personal and social ideals, refinement with citizenship. While from this relationship the idea of justice so important in his earlier conceptions of the larger city would seem to have disappeared, in its rich ambiguity the word "civility" promises to supply that connection too. It embraces not only decency

---

* This and the next line read as follows in the English edition:

> As out of Europe comes a Voice
> Compelling all to make their choice. . . .

The difference between the environmental and volitional formulations in these two versions bears on Auden's religious ideas but not directly on those of the city.

but also, in an archaic theological sense, virtue—a virtue merely of natural or civic goodness but implying the possibility of regeneration. Although in the passage above civility is associated with that civilization we owe first of all to the Greeks, and has therefore in Christian terms a pagan character, like most of the pagan virtues it might be assimilated into the Christian scheme. Thus courage in Cicero became fortitude in Ambrose, temperance became humility or abstinence, and so on. Civility, however, resists such assimilation, etymologically or theologically. It is a most mundane quality, its aristocratic and intellectual elements sharply contrary to the democratic, self-abasing, anti-worldly spirit of traditional Christianity.

It is precisely civility, however, which Auden has most treasured. While he has continued to speak also for justice, his efforts in verse to fuse this moral ideal with his worldly values have worked thus far largely at the level of rhetoric. One looks not just to imagery but to rhetoric in Auden's verse, of course, because he is so emphatically a poet of ideas. Effective as his poems can be, their intellectuality calls for a rational response also. On that ground, his city poems of the last quarter-century show him trying with very incomplete success to unite justice with civility. Thus "New Year Letter" (to cite only some of the many details leading to similar conclusions) resounds with appeals for "the human creature we/Must nurse to sense and decency," for "green and civil life," for "The far interior of our fate/To civilize and to create." The poem reveals Auden's distaste for that post-Renaissance creature "Empiric Economic Man,/The urban, prudent, and inventive," and for "The average of the average man" which "Becomes the dread Leviathan." It expresses the poet's conviction that "Aloneness is man's real condition," and his desire to be instructed

> in the civil art
> Of making from the muddled heart

> A desert and a city where
> The thoughts that have to labor there
> May find locality and peace,
> And pent-up feelings their release. . . .

But where and when and how arrive at this cathartic city? It does not tell us much to speak of Manhattan skyscrapers as "secular cathedrals" or of America as "That culture that had worshiped no/Virgin before the Dynamo. . . ." Those are mildly interesting ideas, but in failing to identify the nature of an appropriate worship or to illumine the question of means they become merely rhetorical. The same defects are to be found in the well-known passage that suggests the feelings behind Auden's expatriation much better than it clarifies what Auden hopes to say:

> More even than in Europe, here
> The choice of patterns is made clear
> With the machine imposes, what
> Is possible and what is not,
> To what conditions we must bow
> In building the Just City now.

In these and many other lines we reach an interpretive impasse. The two cities adjoin in Auden's imagination; as dual emblems of community, order, and ritual they stand well together, but more than these congruities they refuse to yield.

Except, that is, as emblems also of individuality. Whimsical or quirky as it may appear to speak of Auden's cities in this light, it is only paradoxical. A *civitas* of the cultivated few presents, after all, a distinctly individualist ideal, and the evidence of Auden's prose and poetry since about 1940 suggests strongly that Protestant Christianity has always appealed to him partly because it offers a system subject to the individual's assent and with the individual still very much at the center of experience. Stephen Spender has remarked with great acuity that Auden's "problem always has been to discover an authority for the dazzling marginal commentary on existence which is his poems, which is not just himself"; and while one may wish to add to those authorities Spender names—in the early poems Love, then Marxian and other social movements, then the Church—the observation nonetheless holds. Civility and justice are social ideals whose social content may be minimal. They enable the individual to serve ends outside himself without surrendering himself as an end too fully. Difficult as it is to miss this egocentricity in Auden's earlier work, its continuity into the 1940s and after has been obscured by the understandable curiosity about his conversion, and of course also by his massive absorption in the language of religious discourse.

The fact is that Auden has always been attracted to both cities, to the saintly during the period of his putative secularism, as *"Paysage Moralisé"* alone demonstrates, and to the civil continuingly throughout the period of his Christian "commitment." Hence the temptation (not wholly unjustified) to accuse him of intellectual infidelities from one period to the next, hence also the inaccuracy of explaining his ideas in any given year simplistically. A telling feature of his work on religious themes which no one seems to have remarked is that despite its general tone of overwhelming seriousness, he has from time to time been willing to treat Christianity lightly and even ironically. The best instance of this ambiguous treatment is Herod's superb monologue in "The Massacre of the Innocents" section of the Christmas oratorio, "For the Time Being" (written 1941–42). Professor Beach praised this meditation but presumably included it in his dismissal of the oratorio as "propaganda . . . for a sacred cause." Professor Spears, who I think quite rightly admires the oratorio, has praised the speech as "a deft fusion of ancient and modern: Herod is both the historical character and the liberal of the late 1930s. . . . His speech is witty, amusing, and highly persuasive on its own premises: his long struggle to establish law and order and push back superstition is

doomed by this irruption of the Irrational." The wit, however, is turned against the Christians as well as the pagans,
and many features of Herod's civil city are presented quite
attractively—a double complication neither Beach nor Spears
mentions, perhaps because both (for wholly different reasons)
are intent on demonstrating the poet's new religiousness.
Herod describes the Magi as "the trio who came to see me this
morning with an ecstatic grin on their scholarly faces" and a
claim that " 'The world is saved' " on their lips. He foresees
a time ("if this rumour is not stamped out now") when
"Knowledge will degenerate into a riot of subjective visions
—feelings in the solar plexus induced by under-nourishment,
angelic images generated by fevers or drugs, dream warnings
inspired by the sound of falling water."

The forecast that follows of the Christian centuries is cast
entirely in this burlesque mode, ending with Herod's predic-
tion that "the New Aristocracy will consist exclusively of
hermits, bums, and permanent invalids. The Rough Diamond,
the Consumptive Whore, the bandit who is good to his
mother, the epileptic girl who has a way with animals will
be the heroes and heroines of the New Tragedy when the
general, the statesman, and the philosopher have become the
butt of every farce and satire." No matter how devout
Auden's tone on other occasions, here he is plainly enjoying
himself at the expense of an essential religious seriousness.
Herod, moreover, comes off well. He is demoniacally clever,
as Shaw's Don Juan is clever, impressing us with his talents
rather than with the limitations of his views. And in this
speech as elsewhere, Auden reveals a partial sympathy with
those views: besides wit, intelligence and learning, also order,
feeling, decent behavior, "real human excellence."

With loyalties split in just this way, in fine, Auden reveals
himself as both Christian and Roman. His extreme historical
consciousness has from the first led him to comparisons of the
contemporary and ancient worlds, an interest reinforced in the
early 1940s by his enthusiasms for the work of Charles

Williams, Charles N. Cochrane, and Reinhold Niebuhr, all of whom were fascinated with the historic points at which Christianity and secular cultures have touched. The city of Herod's allegiance and Augustine's contempt offered Auden an obvious focus for this interest. As Spears has remarked (in a comment on the *Nones* of 1951), "the state of our own civilization constitutes an inevitable parallel with that of collapsing Rome: both are naturalistic cultures rejecting, in the name of Reason, the Absurd of Christianity . . . ," and Spears quite properly cites in this connection such poems as "The Fall of Rome," "Under Sirius," "The Managers," and "Memorial for the City." What Spears has tended to slight in his glosses on Auden's later work is how very Roman that poet has remained. If the Auden of the postwar years has grown to resemble the chastened yet prideful Augustine, now asserting his own guilt, now condemning the pagan citizenry, he remains at the same time a Juvenal, whom the years have merely gentled. He watches the new Rome fall, therefore, with wholly mixed feelings. Rejoicing should current evils disappear, to be replaced by a Christian age, still he hopes to find an aristocratic civility preserved.

Among his later poems this divided loyalty is best seen in the impressive "Memorial for the City." Again, Spears has brought to light the religious themes, which are undeniably central to the work. Much more remains to be said about this opulent poem, though, more certainly than solitary comment on its 'cities' can supply; but that comment does take us further into it. The manifold cities in the poem serve various roles, not all of them subservient to a religious theme. Auden uses these cities to distinguish broadly two ways of viewing nature, man, and god. There is the *Post-Vergilian City,* with its purposive, religious views, and (by implication) the pre-Vergilian city, the world of Homer, in which earth, gods, and men are perceived as by the crow and camera, naturalistically. The *New City, Sane City, Sinful City, Rational City, Glittering City,* and *Conscious City* of Section II

all refer to dominant social themes or ideals of particular
historical periods, as conceived either within those periods
or by succeeding ones. (My readings here sometimes confirm,
often differ from those of Professor Spears.) Thus *Rational
City* denotes the Enlightenment, particularly as put to work
by the French Revolutionists. The *Sane City* was the ideal
creation of the medieval Scholastics, the *Sinful City* a debasement in practice of that ideal as interpreted by Luther. *Glittering City* is Auden's judgment on that society (presumably
smug, comfortable, commercial) which "denied" or forgot
all those areas of experience the Romantics explored, while
those very explorations are described (in a phrase revealingly
ambiguous rather than simply condemnatory) as having been
undertaken for the *Conscious City*. These cities not only represent, of course, successive historic ideals but also present
alternatives in conduct, as Auden sees them.

The *City* alone, however, as presented in the third and most
important of the four sections, means primarily the ideal of
civilization itself. In this section (reprinted separately in the
Selected Poetry as "Barbed Wire"), the city is described as
having been "abolished." Following the war and of course
more distant causes, the contemporary world has in a sense
become again like Homer's, as the barbed wire runs everywhere, absolutely indifferent to mankind. Coming as this
section does after the review of social ideals from the past,
we may infer that civilization has been destroyed either along
with or because of the disappearance of religious beliefs. And
yet the specific values Auden *names* as having vanished are
not religious but civil:

> Across the plains,
> Between two hills, two villages, two trees, two friends,
> The barbed wire runs which neither argues nor explains
> But where it likes a place, a path, a railroad ends,
> The humor, the cuisine, the rites, the taste,
> The pattern of the City, are erased.

Earlier in the poem we have been prepared for this statement, most explicitly by Auden's attack on what I take to be the post-Reformation bourgeois nationalist world in which proper values have been debased: "Civility a city grown rich. . . ." The recurrent imagery of division in the second and third sections points, moreover, toward the desired restoration of *both* secular and transcendent unities, from the "rival allegiance" of Pope Gregory and Emperor which split the early Christian world so that "The facts, the acts of the City bore a double meaning" on to the barbed wire which has divided men on a worldly plane. Both fractures are to be healed; Auden's ideal is oneness. But what relationship does social health bear to the spiritual? Concluding the barbed-wire section with the line "This is Adam waiting for His City" puts an eloquent period to the religious theme but finesses, in effect, the problem of Auden's own plurality of ideals.

It is, as we have seen, the old problem of the two cities. Attached to both, the poet has been able neither to reconcile them nor relinquish one. Were the metaphysician in him truly pluralistic, he could—as Whitman did, for the most part—have accepted a world of varying values and purposes, conflicts and uncertainties, unresolvable ambiguities. But his hold on experience, like Niebuhr's and that of most of the other intellectuals he has admired, has always demanded singleness and certainty. It has always been our truths *or* yours, domination *or* submission. Confronted by the world as it really is, therefore, he must abandon his dogmatism or attempt to show how experience can, after all, be framed through a single glass. Temperamentally unable to do the first, Auden has long persisted at the second; but the very incompatibility of his own ideals has defeated him. If we remain astonished at the cities he has evoked, it is not because of their ultimate rationality—only because of the skies they illumine.

Epilogue:

The City Today

Most American city writers whose major work has been done since the Second World War give the impression of an intimacy with the metropolis so complete as to deprive them of the capacity for saying anything much about it. This has been true of poets and novelists alike; but because some of the novelists have placed themselves more distinctly or entirely than the poets in relation to an urban milieu, I shall speak only of them in these closing pages.

This perfect familiarity with the city, usually New York, is evident in the best or most interesting fiction of the period—in the work of Saul Bellow, Ralph Ellison, Norman Mailer, Bernard Malamud, James Baldwin, John Updike, J. D. Salinger, Philip Roth, and many others. Even when these writers employ rural, small-town, or primitive settings—as in *Invisible Man, Rabbit, Run,* or *Henderson the Rain King*—we are reminded incessantly of the authors' urbanity of language, technique, or literary knowledge. Dreiser's linguistic solecisms irritated critics a half-century ago; but if the appearance of similar barbarisms in a serious American novel today would be astounding, only a shade less astounding would be the reappearance of a comparable naïveté about the world of the city. Dreiser's sympathy with Carrie's window-gaping or his vision of the city as a fatal trap strike us as out of date or otherwise inappropriate to the cities we know, to the lives we lead in those cities; and so dead are most of us even to the possibility of surprise or sentiment in the city that we find it difficult to understand how James could have thought that the widespread notion of Paris as morally destructive might work either for or against him in *The Ambassadors*. Now all the great, uniform cities—particularly the American ones, which have remained by and large impervious to individuation—would seem to have lost whatever power they once had to arouse awe or dread, or to address anyone in a distinctive idiom. They simply are *there*—measureless, prodigious, blank.

One thinks immediately of apparent exceptions. The Manhattan of Bellow's *The Victim*, for example, is rendered in considerable detail of the following sort:

> There was still a redness in the sky, like the flame at the back of a vast baker's oven; the day hung on, gaping fierily over the black of the Jersey shore. The Hudson had a low luster, and the sea was probably no more numbing in its cold, Leventhal imagined, than the subway under his feet was in its heat; the trains rushing by under the gratings and along the slanting brown rock walls seemed to set off charges of metal dust.

Even in this novel, however, much of the description would apply as well to Chicago or Los Angeles or perhaps Houston; and Bellow continually widens his urban frame of reference by comparisons of New York to Bangkok and Singapore, by allusions such as that to New Yorkers as "the children of Caliban," and by his firmly allegorical conception of the conflict between the main characters, Leventhal and Allbee. Indeed, as Marcus Klein has shown in an exceedingly acute essay (reprinted in *After Alienation*, 1964), Bellow's is a "city imagination" by virtue of its representation of a New York and Chicago "dense with neighbors and noise, with streetcars, subways, families, friends, soot, and filth," but

more importantly in its metaphorical use of these particulars
to evoke the clutter, the chaos, the burdensome "things" of
contemporary American life. The neighbors and noise matter,
but what they mean—or fail to mean—matters a good deal
more. "Things were too complex," Tommy Wilhelm thinks
to himself in *Seize the Day,* "but they might be reduced to
simplicity again. Recovery was possible. First he had to get
out of the city."

For reasons dictated by the megalopolitan culture they
know and by their own imaginations, most of these novelists
follow in some way the prescription Tommy Wilhelm gives
for his own recovery. First they get out of the city, sometimes
by sending their heroes away—Henderson to Africa, Augie
March to Mexico, Malamud's Levin out West to a new life
as different and remote as possible from the one he had known
in New York, or Roy Hobbs (in *The Natural*) out on the
road with the baseball team. Sometimes they get out of the
city by bending its reality to the demands of a surreality, as
Ellison does in *Invisible Man;* or by refusing, as Malamud
refuses in *The Assistant* and Baldwin in *Another Country,* to
make the urban environment really substantial; or simply by
choosing locales outside the city altogether, as Updike does
in *The Poorhouse Fair* and *The Centaur.* The quests of these
heroes and of their authors are for fresh starts, for adjustment
to the natural laws of conduct, for self-assertion, for making
amends, for knowledge, for a score of other ends comparably
private and individual. Discovering how far and in what
respects these ends involve a rejection of the city, as they
appear to, is a task with its own intricacies and wonders, now
left for another time.

Suggested Readings

Auden, W. H., *The Enchafèd Flood; or, the Romantic Iconography of the Sea.* New York, Random House, 1950. *Excitingly aphoristic and wide-ranging comment on recurrent images in modern literature, such as the sea, desert, garden, and city.*

Baird, James, *Ishmael.* Baltimore, Johns Hopkins Press, 1956. *Though a trifle inconclusive and murky, a frequently suggestive study of primitivist archetypes in Melville and many others. Chapter XIV takes up "The Infernal City."*

Beach, Joseph Warren, *Obsessive Images: Symbolism in Poetry of the 1930's and 1940's.* Minneapolis, University of Minnesota Press, 1960. *Posthumous and not wholly finished, this detailed survey nevertheless has considerable value as both literary history and criticism. Deals with isolated symbols and with symbolic patterns repeated from poet to poet: for example, Auden's islands and cities.*

Fanger, Donald, *Dostoevsky and Romantic Realism: A Study of Dostoevsky in Relation to Balzac, Dickens, and Gogol.* Cambridge, Harvard University Press, 1965. *An intelligent and informed scrutiny of the four writers' "obsessive concern" with the changing quality of human life under the metropolitan pressures of Paris, London, or Petersburg.*

Klein, Marcus, *After Alienation: American Novels in Mid-Century.* Cleveland and New York, World Publishing Company, 1964. *Penetrating essays on Bellow, Ellison, Baldwin, Morris, and Malamud, displaying sensitivity to the specifically urban character of much of their fiction, particularly that of Bellow.*

Marx, Leo, *The Machine in the Garden: Technology and the Pastoral Ideal in America.* New York, Oxford University Press, 1964. *An extremely lucid interpretation of the conflict of industrial with pastoral motifs in American literature and culture. The occasional allusions to an urban mythology might well provide starting-points for a comparably broad inquiry into the imaginative impact of the city beyond that suggested by the present volume.*

Weimer, David R., ed., *City and Country in America*. New York, Appleton-Century-Crofts, 1962. *An anthology of agrarian, urbanist, and regionalist thought, exemplifying the work of Kropotkin, Ruskin, Henry George, and others whose visions of 'the city' have yet to be explored on their imaginative side.*

INDEX

Adams, Henry, 5
Algren, Nelson, v
Allen, Gay Wilson, 28
Anderson, Quentin, 10
Auden, Erika Mann, 129
Auden, W. H., 123–43; *The Capital*, 131–2; *The Dyer's Hand*, 130; *The Enchafèd Flood*, 129n, 147; *The Fall of Rome*, 141; *For the Time Being*, 139–40; *Look, Stranger!*, 124; *The Managers*, 141; *Memorial for the City*, 141–3; *New Year Letter*, 133–8; *Nones*, 141; *Paysage Moralisé*, 125–8, 129, 139; *Poems* (1930), 123; *The Shield of Achilles*, 11; *Spain 1937*, 128–9, 135; *The Unknown Citizen*, 131; *Venus Will Now Say a Few Words*, 123
Augustine, Saint, 127–9, 141

Baird, James, 147
Baldwin, James, 144, 146
Balzac, Honoré de, vi
Baudelaire, Pierre Charles, 10, 15, 20–1, 22
Beach, Joseph Warren, 123–8, 139–40, 147
Bellow, Saul, 3, 144–6
Berryman, John, 55
Bishop, Elizabeth, vi
Blake, William, 5
Brancusi, Constantin, 85, 87
Breton, André, 86
Brooks, Van Wyck, 89
Broun, Heywood, 100
Brown, Charles Brockden, vi
Burchard, John, 5–6
Byron, George Gordon, Lord, 129

Cambon, Glauco, 105
Cézanne, Paul, 62, 85

Chase, Richard, 55
Cochrane, Charles N., 141
Conrad, Joseph, 77
Cowley, Malcolm, 95
Crane, Hart, v
Crane, Stephen, 2, 6, 10, 13, 52–64, 65, 84; *The Blue Hotel*, 61; *An Episode of War*, 57; *An Experiment in Misery*, 57; *George's Mother*, 56, 59–60, 61; *Maggie*, 9, 52–7, 58, 59, 61, 132n; *The Men in the Storm*, 57; *The Monster*, 61; *The Open Boat*, 61; *The Red Badge of Courage*, 57–8, 59, 61
Cummings, E. E., 8, 12, 78–87, 89, 114; *& [AND]*, 85; *Tulips and Chimneys*, 85

Dickens, Charles, vi
Dos Passos, John, v
Dostoevsky, F. M., vi
Dreiser, Theodore, 6, 13, 41, 51, 65–77, 81–2, 89–90, 102–3, 144–5; *An American Tragedy*, 67, 132n; *The Bulwark*, 67; *The "Genius,"* 67, 69, 72–3; *Sister Carrie*, 9, 65–7
Duchamp, Marcel, 85
Dudley, Dorothy, 69

Edwards, Jonathan, 1–2
Eliot, T. S., v, 20–1, 32, 78, 104, 118
Ellison, Ralph, 144, 146
Emerson, Ralph Waldo, 21–2, 75, 79, 112, 114, 133

Fanger, Donald, vi, 147
Farrell, James T., v
Faulkner, William, 71, 84, 89
Fiedler Leslie, 25, 25n

Fitzgerald, F. Scott, 9, 12, 13, 88–103; *Babylon Revisited*, 3, 93, 101; *The Beautiful and Damned*, 91–3, 102; *Crazy Sunday*, 94, 99; *The Great Gatsby*, 93, 100–1; *The Ice Palace*, 99; *The Last Tycoon*, 90, 93, 96–8, 99, 101–2; *Magnetism*, 94; *My Lost City*, 7–8, 102–3; *The Rich Boy*, 101; *Tender Is the Night*, 90, 93, 94 95–6, 97, 98, 101; *This Side of Paradise*, 88, 93, 100

Frost, Robert, 104
Fussell, Paul, Jr., vi

Gilson, Étienne, 128–9
Ginsberg, Allen, 122
Gogh, Vincent van, 62
Gogol, Nikolai V., vi

Handlin, Oscar, 5–6
Hardy, Thomas, 77
Hawthorne, Nathaniel, vi, 4, 67–8
Heal, Edith, 112
Hemingway, Ernest, 57–8, 61, 95
Hopper, Edward, 69
Howells, William Dean, 52, 53–5, 58, 79, 87, 90

James, Henry, 10, 12, 13, 34–51, 65, 67, 69, 71, 79, 84, 89, 101; *The Ambassadors*, 3, 4, 9, 35, 39, 46–51, 145; *The American*, 4, 38–42, 42n; *The American Scene*, 4, 42; *The Aspern Papers*, 42n; *The Beast in the Jungle*, 42n; *The Bostonians*, 42, 42n; *Daisy Miller*, 4, 37; *The Europeans*, 42, 42n; *In the Cage*, 42n; *An International Episode*, 42n;

Italian Hours, 42; *The Portrait of a Lady*, 4, 43–6; *The Princess Casamassima*, 4, 42n; *Roderick Hudson*, 35–8, 40–2, 43; *Tales of Three Cities*, 42; *The Tragic Muse*, 42n; *Transatlantic Sketches*, 42; *Washington Square*, 42, 42n; *The Wings of the Dove*, 42n, 43

Jarrell, Randall, 11n, 17n
Joyce, James, 119

Kafka, Franz, 10, 61–4, 84
Kaiser, Georg, 60
Kaufman, G. S., 60
Kazin, Alfred, 69
Keats, John, 25–6
Klein, Marcus, 145–6, 147

Lawrence, D. H., 12–13, 44, 77, 98–9
Lewis, R. W. B., 29

McCartney, Anne, vi
MacNeice, Louis, 129
Mailer, Norman, 102, 144
Malamud, Bernard, 144, 146
Marks, Barry, 84–5
Marx, Leo, 147
Matisse, Henri, 62, 85, 86
Matthiessen, F. O., 15, 20, 69
Melville, Herman, vi, 2, 3, 53, 67, 69, 88–9
Millay, Edna St. Vincent, 10n
Mizener, Arthur, 94, 97
Munch, Edvard, 62

Niebuhr, Reinhold, 141, 143
Nietzsche, F. W., 133
Nolde, Emil, 62
Norris, Frank, vi

O'Neill, Eugene, 60
Orwell, George, 57

Paul, David, 20*n*
Peck, A. L., 5*n*
Perkins, Maxwell, 99
Poe, Edgar Allan, 3–4
Pound, Ezra, 104

Quinn, Sister M. Bernetta, 118

Rilke, Rainer Maria, 5
Roth, Philip, 144

Salinger, J. D., 144
Schorske, Carl E., 5
Shaw, Bernard, 140
Shelley, Percy B., 25
Sloan, John, 69
Soares, Lota de Maçedo, vi
Spears, Monroe K., 128, 139–40, 141–2
Spender, Stephen, 138–9
Spilka, Mark, vi
Stieglitz, Alfred, 69
Strindberg, August, 60

Thoreau, Henry David, 21–2, 114
Twain, Mark, 89

Updike, John, 144, 146

Walcutt, Charles C., 60–2
Wells, Henry, 117
West, Nathanael, 102
White, Lucia, 3–6
White, Morton, 3–6
Whitman, Walt, 6–9, 11, 13, 14–33, 58, 69, 75, 78–9, 87, 114, 143; *A Broadway Pageant*, 30–2; *Chants Democratic*, 29; *Crossing Brooklyn Ferry*, 7, 23–6, 28, 35; *Democratic Vistas*, 7–8, 27–8, 43; *Drum-Taps*, 34; *Enfans d'Adam*, 15–16; *First O Songs for a Prelude*, 34–5; *Leaves of Grass*, 15, 16, 35; *Mannahatta*, 22–3; *Out of the Cradle, Endlessly Rocking*, 15; *The Ox-Tamer*, 21–2; *Passage to India*, 15; *Pioneers! O Pioneers!*, 30; *Salut au Monde!*, 7, 17–18; *Song of Myself*, 2, 15, 16–17, 21; *Song of the Open Road*, 7, 18–20; *Song of the Redwood Tree*, 32; *Specimen Days*, 14, 22, 26–7; *Unnamed Lands*, 29
Williams, Charles, 140–1
Williams, William Carlos, 6, 10–11, 14–15, 78, 104–22; *The Flower*, 104, 105–7, 109; *The Host*, 116; *A Morning Imagination of Russia*, 114–16; *Paterson*, 13, 104, 105, 116–22; *Perfection*, 112; *Perpetuum Mobile: The City*, 8–9, 109–12; *A Place (Any Place) to Transcend All Places*, 113–14; *Raleigh Was Right*, 112; *To a Friend Concerning Several Ladies*, 108–9
Wilson, Edmund, 103
Wordsworth, William, 15, 129
Wright, James, 5–6